My First Year in Book Publishing

MY FIRST YEAR
IN
BOOK
PUBLISHING

REAL-WORLD
STORIES
FROM

AMERICA'S BOOK
PUBLISHING
PROFESSIONALS

Edited By

LISA HEALY

WALKER AND COMPANY
NEW YORK

First published in the United States of America in 1994 by Walker Publishing
Company, Inc.

Published simultaneously in Canada by Thomas Allen & Son Canada, Limited,
Markham, Ontario

Library of Congress Cataloging-in-Publication Data
My first year in book publishing : real-world stories from America's
book publishing professionals / edited by Lisa Healy.
p.   cm.
ISBN 0-8027-1294-0. —ISBN 0-8027-7425-3 (pbk.)
I. Publishers and publishing—United States—Biography.
I.   Healy, Lisa.
Z473.M98   1994
070.5′092′273—dc20
[B]   94-9607
CIP

"Ignorance and Curiosity" by Robert B. Wyatt was initially published in
American Bookseller.

Book design by Glen M. Edelstein

Printed in the United States of America

2   4   6   8   10   9   7   5   3   I

To my mother

Contents

FOREWORD: THE MAGIC IS IN THE MYSTERIES   *Samuel S. Vaughan*   ix

ACKNOWLEDGMENTS   xiii

INTRODUCTION   *Lisa Healy*   xv

1. Interested in a Career in Book Publishing?
   Gregory Giangrande   1

2. Take the Book!   *Laura J. Blake*   10

3. Of Filing Cabinets and Publishers' Invoices
   Jane von Mehren   16

4. I Didn't Get a Degree from Berkeley for
   This!   *Kimberly Wiar*   24

5. The Accidental Profession   *Andrea Cascardi*   30

6. "You Might Like This; It Is Very Good"   *Joy Smith*   35

7. If You Won the Lottery   *Sylvia K. Miller*   44

8. First Steps   *Victoria Klose*   56

9. Beautiful Enough to Be Unnoticed
   Claire Naylon Vaccaro   65

10. Blessed and Cursed   *Elyse Dubin*   74

11. Enter Indexer   *Sydney Wolfe Cohen*   86

12. What Is a Cash Cow, Anyway?   *Thomas S. Novak*   93

13. Willing to Be Lucky   *Kristin Kliemann*   100

14. Dancing School   *Maryann Palumbo*   110

15. Hey, Lady, Ya Wanna Buy a Book? *or* My First Year
    as a Traveling Book Salesman   *Gregory Brandenburgh*   118

16. Champagne Corks and Mafia Killers
    William Parkhurst   127

17. Ignorance and Curiosity   *Robert B. Wyatt*   145

BIBLIOGRAPHY   153

INDEX   155

Foreword: The Magic Is in the Mysteries

SAMUEL S. VAUGHAN

YOUR FIRST "YEAR"

Here are some episodes and insights to help you in your first year in publishing. In this book, some of the best book people offer anecdotes and antidotes and advice. Think of it as a guide, or survival manual, for life in the boot camp of books.

Your first year is apt to be one of fear, joy, awkwardness, confusion, delightful surprises, disillusioning realities, tests even before you've been taught. Unless you've attended one of the preparatory institutes for publishing or were raised in a publishing family (if you can call the chairman "Dad," ignore these remarks), you are not likely to know even the vocabulary, the shorthand that passes for English in the day-to-day operations of a publishing company. In many ways your first year will be one of the most difficult years. But don't worry: There will be a few even more difficult years ahead, years in which you will be able to speak the language and can complain like a pro.

Your "first year" will not be a year at all, of course. Life doesn't play out, as we say these days, in neat twelve-month packages, any more than history occurs by decades, no matter how often television programs and magazines insist that it does. But somewhere in the first ten minutes or the first twenty months or so, you'll decide that publishing is or is not for you. You'll have passed that point before you realize it, and you'll be deep into the next phase, which is really learning your trade.

Which is it—trade, job, craft, career, profession, art . . . ? Publishing is a business, you'll be told, over and over. If a house doesn't succeed as a business, over the long term, its people cannot be good publishers or poor publishers; they will be extinct publishers. But publishing at its best is more than a business, and eventually you might find that you have more than a mere job or career. You'll have a vocation, one at the busy intersection of commerce and culture, education and scholarship, literature and journalism, entertainment and art.

Your first year is apt to be spent in the ancient apprenticeship system. That puts a premium on the person you're working for. If starting salaries seem low, remember that you are in the business of barter: your services in exchange for a chance to learn from a woman or a man who wants to teach you, or at least give you the opportunity to learn. Some companies have excellent training programs; most are still sadly haphazard. A fine editor, Kate Medina, at Random House, is a marvelous mentor. Her advice? If you don't draw a boss who aids in your development, *leave.*

Your obligation is to make your boss's job easier. (My father, who worked in a shipyard during World War I, taught me that a good helper doesn't get a wrench when asked; he produces the right wrench before being asked.) Put yourself in the boss's place; anticipate needs. Then, when you're ready, you can fill the boss's place, instead of just his or her coffee cup.

The boss's job, as part of the bargain, is to teach, by example and by giving you opportunities. Or letting you see and seize them.

MY FIRST YEAR

As you contemplate your first year in publishing, I am looking forward to my forty-second year. We have much in common. I still have a lot to learn. And every year is like the first year in a few respects: anticipation, certainties and confusion, frustrations and fun, frequently unrealistic expectations (on your part and by authors, agents, marketers, mothers, business managers, Significant Others, sales departments, executives, Insignificant Others, et al.) and yet serendipitous successes. Publishing is fatiguing and at the same time self-renewing.

In my earliest years, I sometimes sat at my desk and looked at the résumés of others out there in the waiting room, from "better" schools, with better credentials, trying to get a job. What, I wondered, was I doing here while they were out there, waiting?

Well, maybe it was luck. Or need, drive, a suitable ambition, a willingness to work—and remember, no matter how attractive certain occupations are, at base there is always a great deal of work. Or maybe I just managed to come up with the right wrench at the right time. Without waiting to be asked.

There are still mysteries in publishing for me, too. I've learned from some of the best, the men and women who were my mentors—and from my assistants.

Publishing is change and constancy, a froth of the new, over the mysteries of the depths. Underneath the chaotic, roiled surface of CD-ROMs and "media mergers" is a process I think of as classic publishing. It involves performing the duties of our calling—reading, financing, editing, designing, printing, selling, distributing, and more—in ways that would have been recognizable to Aldus Manutius, who some say was the first modern editor-publisher-printer in fifteenth-century Florence.

Mysteries? Still? Sure. Easy ones, among them: What is art? What is history? What, why, and how do people read? What is our need for stories—a mark of the cultivated person or, as I believe, a hunger as basic as that for bread? Who is the "public" (or the publics)? What changes in the culture and in the commerce are likely to be enduring, and which are only today's passing fancies?

But the mysteries are part of the magic.

And welcome to them.

Samuel S. Vaughan is currently editor-at-large for Random House, Inc., William Morrow, and W. W. Norton. Some of his previous positions include president/publisher and editor-in-chief at Doubleday and senior vice president and editor at Random House. He also served as chairman of the Education for Publishing Committee of the Association of American Publishers and was the principal author of a report on the education and development of publishing people called The Accidental Profession.

Acknowledgments

The people who wrote the essays collected here are due all the credit for this book's existence. Some have been my friends for years; others were strangers until I approached them to ask a favor. All are offered my undying gratitude and a copy of the book, which I hope they will enjoy. I'd also like to thank my friends and colleagues who volunteered to tell their stories, who suggested possible contributors, and who provided enthusiastic support.

It has been a pleasure to work with the professionals at Walker and Company. I'd particularly like to thank Ramsey Walker, president, whose first year in book publishing was spent, not surprisingly, at Walker and Company; and my editors, Mary Kennan Herbert, who began her career in publishing at Prentice Hall as a junior copywriter in the college advertising department, and Sarah Collins, assistant editor, who began as an editorial assistant at Walker and Company. I also appreciate the efforts of the various other publishing professionals who helped produce this book: Julia O'Day, information systems technician; Beena Kamlani, who made her editorial debut at Harper & Row; Vicki Haire, copy editor, who began her career as a copywriter at John Wiley and Company; Glen Edelstein, interior designer, who began as a design associate at Random House, College Division; Debbie Glasserman, jacket designer, who began as a graphic artist at Facts On File, Inc.; and Sydney Wolfe Cohen, president of S. W. Cohen & Associates, indexer, whose story appears here.

Introduction

There has never been a more exciting time to enter the profession of book publishing. Recent advances in computer technology are changing the nature of book publishing as radically as the technological advance of Johannes Gutenberg's movable type changed the process of disseminating text more than five hundred years ago. It has become necessary not only to redefine what we mean by the word "book" and by "publishing" as a whole but also to invent language to encompass a variety of new electronic media.

This imminent revolution will expand our ability to offer information in both nontextual and textual formats. Reading will remain one of the most effective and efficient means of accessing data. Something resembling books as we've known them for generations will always have a place in human communications. It seems reasonable to expect that much of the basic trade lore, the traditional body of knowledge of book publishing, will remain essentially unchanged and that the nature of entry-level jobs, the

traditional apprenticeships of the profession, will adapt gradually
to change in the industry.

First jobs in book publishing, as in other industries, often involve a certain amount of work that is less than glamorous. Yet
publishing remains a challenging, creative, stimulating activity.
This book describes through a variety of voices a diverse range of
careers in publishing and shows why the profession continues to
attract some of the finest talents emerging from our colleges and
universities today. Though young publishing professionals may
lose a few illusions along the way, it is remarkable that people
manage to retain so much of the idealistic vision that brought
them into the profession initially. A love of books, of words and
ideas seems impervious to the passage of time and the vicissitudes
of the working world.

There is no quintessential first year in book publishing, no one
story that can distill, let alone predict, another person's experience
of entering a career. There's no average publishing company any
more than there is a typical book. The Association of American
Publishers reports that in the United States alone, 74,000 people
work in book publishing. Two thousand companies deemed by
the AAP to be "consistently active" are complemented by many
institutional and governmental presses and smaller private firms.
The 1993 edition of *The Literary Market Place* includes data on
3,686 publishers that produce on average at least three books a
year. These companies currently publish about 50,000 different
books each year.

The only common denominator among the tens of thousands
of people working in publishing is a love of books, a theme that
echoes throughout this collection of autobiographical essays.
Rather than constituting a representative sample, the contributors
to this volume were selected in an effort to highlight the tremendous variety of career opportunities available in book publishing.

In the following pages, you will read the personal stories of more than a dozen successful publishing professionals of all ages. They grew up in towns and cities from the West Coast to the East, from Michigan to Texas, from Oklahoma to New Hampshire. You'll hear from people who began in publishing as soon as they graduated from college (or even before) and from more mature career changers who explored other professions before finding their homes in the book publishing world. You'll read the personal stories of people who launched their careers in Boston, in Chicago, in San Francisco, and in the world capital of publishing, New York. Philadelphia, Washington, D.C., Los Angeles and San Diego, and many other metropolitan areas offer a range of publishing activities. Some cities are rich in career opportunities; though, of course, in other communities a job hunter may find fewer options. Living and working in New York is by no means a prerequisite for a successful publishing career. Academic institutions around the country support publishing communities as well. Publishing is expected to become increasingly less centralized as the latest electronic media make communications in general easier, faster, and more flexible.

The professionals whose stories are presented here debuted in a variety of publishing houses: a university press, a small independent publisher, a religious publisher, a reference book publisher, and the powerful multinational conglomerates that aim at the best-seller list with trade books—hardcover and paperback books intended to appeal to a wide general audience of both children and adults.

Beyond the trade books that fill the shelves of the typical bookstore and public library, the publishing industry produces elementary school, high school, and college textbooks and other educational materials; scholarly works from university presses; specialized works for professionals in law or accounting, for instance, and science, technology, and medicine (STM); religious publications; general reference works such as encyclopedias and dictionaries; book club editions and other mail-order offerings; and an increasingly broad array of ancillary products such as audiotapes of books.

The physical format of books and the way in which books are distributed create additional variety in the book business. Many hardcover books are reprinted in lower-priced editions called trade paperbacks or quality paperbacks, which are distributed to bookstores in much the same way as hardcovers are. Trade paperbacks can as easily be original publications as reprints and are available in a range of sizes and prices, as are hardcover books. A third format, mass-market paperbacks, can also be original works or reprints. They're less expensive than trade paperbacks, are designed to a standard "rack size," and are widely disseminated through magazine distribution channels to bookstores, newsstands, drugstores, convenience stores, supermarkets, airports, and so on. Many publishing people feel quite comfortable working in all three formats, while others tend to specialize in a particular market.

These stories of the lives of publishing people at the beginning of their careers illustrates only a few of myriad career possibilities available to people who love books and who value the personal rewards that come from playing a part in the culturally crucial task of making reading material available to society.

An unusually rich source of essayists has been the faculty of New York University's Certificate in Book Publishing program at the School of Continuing Education. Because these contributors interact regularly with people who are new to the publishing scene, they are able to zero in on the precise concerns of today's budding publishers. Like his faculty colleagues, Gregory Giangrande is so enthusiastic about working in publishing that he gives his personal time to share that enthusiasm with students at NYU and elsewhere.

Greg's essay, "Interested in a Career in Book Publishing?" grows out of his years of experience at Random House, where he began as a college recruiter asking that question and where he is now the manager of human resources. During his first year on the job, most of it spent touring the country scouting out the industry's most crucial asset, human resources, Greg learned a great deal about identifying people who have the potential to become good publishers and about developing that talent. As an expert on the first year in book publishing, Greg offers observations that illuminate a broad range of entry-level situations. His role as a human resources administrator is also of primary importance in a discussion of publishing careers because half of all publishing employees in the United States work in administration and operations, providing indispensable support to the 25 percent of people who are employed in marketing and publicity, the 15 percent who comprise the editorial staff, and the 10 percent who handle production.

Before encountering these marketers, editors, and production people, we'll detour outside the publishing house itself to meet the literary agent who introduces the author to his or her publisher and who represents the writer's interests in all subsequent dealings. The agent submits the author's work to appropriate editors, negotiates the deal, irons out the contract, follows through by keeping an eye on the publishing process, and does much more. Although agents are usually not involved in transactions with small presses or with university presses, they are crucial to both authors and the editors at the larger houses who publish trade books, those targeted at a general readership.

Laura J. Blake, an agent at the distinguished firm of Curtis Brown, Ltd., is unusual among authors' representatives in that she discovered her calling while still in college. Many people hoping to enter the publishing business are unaware of the importance of an agent's role in trade book publishing and don't include this job possibility in their initial search. Consequently, many of today's agents began their careers in-house, working in various capacities, most commonly, it seems, on the editorial side. Editors (and others) have been known to find agenting an appealing career option for several reasons. Most literary agencies are tiny operations in comparison to the publishers with whom they deal; the atmosphere in an agency tends to be entrepreneurial and noncorporate. Another major difference is in the pay structure of the two employment opportunities; whereas editors enjoy regular paychecks, which increase only gradually, agents work on commission. There's not much of a safety net beyond the salaried entry-level slots in agencies, but there's also no ceiling on potential earnings. Among the wealthiest people in publishing today are the agents who represent best-selling authors. But it takes a lot of work—and some luck—to get to that level of success. Laura is off to a great start, as you'll see in her essay, "Take the Book!"

The publishing people with whom agents have the closest relationships are the acquiring editors (also called acquisitions editors), who generally begin their careers as editorial assistants. An agent working on commission makes no money until a contract is negotiated. In most instances, an acquiring editor, often even a relatively young editor, exercises what amounts to veto power for the imprint. Therefore, one of the most important decisions an agent makes is choosing the editor or editors to whom a manuscript or book proposal will be submitted. The choice of a particular editor will also have a significant effect on the way the book is published. The agent-editor relationship is central to the careers of both people since an acquiring editor is measured by the performance of the books he or she attracts from agents. If an editor wants to see the best material available, the editor needs to convince agents that he or she is the best possible person at the best possible house to publish this book (of course, the ability to offer large sums of money can influence the situation).

One of the best editors is executive editor Jane von Mehren of Penguin Books. Jane is an award-winning editor of award-winning fiction and nonfiction writers, many of whom have enjoyed commercial success as well as critical acclaim. In NYU's Certificate in Book Publishing program she teaches a course that details not only the acquisitions process but also the many other activities performed by the acquiring editor during the publication process. In her essay, "Of Filing Cabinets and Publishers' Invoices," she recounts her early exploration of the many roles of editorial people, junior and senior.

Editors need a good understanding of the entire publishing process from beginning to end because they play such a central role in deciding which books will be published and how the books will be shaped editorially. Editors also introduce each book to all the other people who will be involved in its publication. The editor's vision of the book informs the art director's concept of the jacket, shapes the publicist's pitch, focuses the initial discussion of the marketing strategy, and strongly colors the sales force's perception of the book. But many editors, it seems, remain basically ignorant about the last step in delivering a book to a reader. During Jane's first year in book publishing, she worked nights at the Traveller's Bookstore, an invaluable learning experience that might be recommended to any publishing professional. Another, different experience as an entry-level bookseller is offered later in this collection.

The acquisitions editor recommends the stronger, more promising projects to the editor-in-chief or editorial director and subsequently to the publisher (although in many instances the job titles are synonymous). Acquisitions procedures vary from one trade house to another and are different at university presses and for publishers of professional material, but generally the decision to commit significant resources to publishing a project is made after a lot of discussion among a lot of people. Usually, the final call is the publisher's (or director's), as is the responsibility for subsequent major decisions concerning the book's publication. Jane von Mehren's essay on her apprenticeship with senior editor James O'Shea Wade of Crown Publishers is followed by those of Kimberly Wiar, who began her career as secretary to the director of a notable university press, and of Andrea Cascardi, who spent part of her first year in book publishing as an editorial assistant to an editor-in-chief of children's books.

Kimberly Wiar, an acquisitions editor at the University of Oklahoma Press, began her career as secretary to Morris Philipson, still the director of the University of Chicago Press. As a young woman hoping to be an acquisitions editor one day, in her first job Kim was well placed to get an overview of publishing. In addition to offering the view from inside the publisher's office, Kim's story of university press publishing, "I Didn't Get a Degree from Berkeley for This!" provides a contrast to the trade publishing world and broadens our geographical reach well beyond the East Coast. Kim didn't expect to begin her career in Chicago, but, as it turned out, she couldn't have picked a better place.

Up next is Andrea Cascardi, now the associate publisher of Hyperion Books for Children, part of the Walt Disney Company, Inc., who didn't want to be an acquiring editor. In fact, when she graduated from college, she thought she was destined to write for magazines rather than publish books. As she relates in her story, "The Accidental Profession," she held two jobs during her first year in book publishing, finding her niche on the second try, as editorial assistant to the editor-in-chief of Houghton Mifflin children's books in Boston. Her peregrinations provide an inside perspective on both marketing and editing children's books. Children's book publishing is a strong segment of the industry and, as Andrea points out, a special one because children's lives are transformed when they get excited about reading. Nothing else in publishing quite compares to providing books for this challenging special market. Since children are not the people who actually buy most children's books, children's book editors and marketers must learn how to appeal simultaneously to the adults with disposable income and the end consumers, the kids. This dual market requires a children's book publisher to stay in touch with the child inside his or her own adult self. It's a way of life that works beautifully for Andrea, even if her career was an accident.

If the acquiring editor's recommendation to publish is approved by the editor-in-chief and the publisher (and any other relevant decision makers), the editor makes an offer to the author's agent to acquire the right to publish the book. The editor sometimes has to compete against editors at other houses who also want to sign up the project. The editor and the agent strike a deal; the author signs the contract; and the editor works with the writer to perfect the manuscript—in an ideal world. Of course, in real life, nothing is ever that simple. But sooner or later the editor declares the work ready for production, the next major phase of the book publishing process. The acquiring editor fills out a thousand forms dealing with a million details of the book and passes the manuscript and the illustrations to the managing editor, who oversees a department often known as "production editorial" or "editorial production."

Joy Smith, formerly an associate editor in the trade department at Charles Scribner's Sons, spent her first year in book publishing assisting the managing editor of Pantheon Books and Schocken Books, two imprints of Random House, Inc. The managing editor has the awesome responsibility of coordinating additional editorial activities with the work of designers and manufacturers. And he or she has to do it on a tight and increasingly inflexible schedule because the manuscript came in late from the overworked editor because it was delivered late by the author. In her essay, "You Might Like This; It Is Very Good," Joy tells us how much she learned by interacting with the editorial, design, and production people at Pantheon, then under the direction of Andre Schiffrin, a provocative and socially conscious publisher of distinction.

Joy offers an additional perspective essential to any discussion of careers in book publishing by relating her experience as a person who doesn't fit the dominant demographic profile of publishers. Although women in publishing hold few of the highest positions, they are very much in evidence everywhere else in the business; there are many female vice presidents heading departments. Unfortunately, the same is not true for people of color. This is one reason why Joy chose her career, as you'll learn.

A few floors away from Joy Smith's office in Scribner trade editorial was senior editor Sylvia K. Miller's domain in Scribner reference. The two women, who were not acquainted with each other before having contributed essays to this book, both traveled from a West Coast university to an East Coast summer publishing course to an entry-level job assisting a managing editor. They both faced financial constraints and relate stories of the challenge of finding affordable (and livable) housing in New York. A few years later, they were both acquiring editors at the same publishing house, but their professional lives are worlds apart.

Sylvia Miller recounts in her essay, "If You Won the Lottery," how delighted she was to land her first job as secretary to acquiring editor Lloyd Chilton and managing editor Elyse Dubin of Macmillan's Professional and Reference Books Division. She learned a tremendous amount from both of her first mentors before she discovered her fascination with the development of thematic encyclopedias and dictionaries and other multivolume reference sets. She now manages to combine her talents in editorial production and in acquisitions for Scribner's and considers herself privileged to be able to support scholars and scholarship by providing substantial, definitive summaries of whole fields of knowledge.

Managing editors and production editors, as Joy and Sylvia write, coordinate the work of copy editors, proofreaders, indexers, designers, and manufacturing specialists. Among the unsung heroes and heroines of the editorial production world are the copy editors, whose diligent work may go unnoticed until an author becomes upset, rightly or wrongly, about a suggested change or an innocent query. But a writer or an acquiring editor who truly understands and respects the language will always value the ability of a good copy editor to fine-tune a manuscript and to do it diplomatically. As we'll learn from Victoria Klose's essay, "First Steps," a copy editor, often working freelance, receives a "final" manuscript; she then corrects grammar, spelling, punctuation, and syntax, conforming the manuscript to house style; ensures clarity, rhetorical effectiveness, and consistency; and undertakes light fact checking. The copy editor queries the author and/or editor in the margins of the manuscript concerning any other editorial issues, and the author and editor respond with a last round of changes before the manuscript moves to the compositor to be set in type.

Most authors and many editors need a lot more help from copy editors than they realize. Though they're not alchemists, copy editors can and often do take on an apparently hopeless muddle and turn it into a good book and make a good manuscript an even better book. It's a challenging task but a satisfying one. And it takes a person who is not just careful and diplomatic; the copy editor must also be steeped in the language and culturally erudite.

When Tory writes about copyediting, she writes not only from personal experience of the craft but also as someone who has supervised the work of dozens of in-house and freelance editors and who has taught copyediting and proofreading to hundreds of NYU students.

While the copy editor is busy polishing the language in one copy of the manuscript, another copy has been sent to the design department where decisions will be made about the visual elements of the book. Book designers and jacket designers can work either in-house or as freelancers. Sometimes the person who designs the inside of the book will also design the jacket or cover; sometimes the jacket will be designed by a different designer. Often a third person will provide the art—a painting, an illustration, a photograph—for the cover.

Every reader is aware of the book cover, but relatively few people appreciate the work that goes into designing the inside of the book. Our inside view of book design has been provided by Claire Naylon Vaccaro, who began her career as a design assistant at Alfred A. Knopf and who now, seven years later, runs her own business working for many different publishers designing a variety of books. Her essay, "Beautiful Enough to Be Unnoticed," offers a revealing look at the subtle art of book design and details the many decisions a designer has to make as he or she sits down in front of a blank page to create an appropriate visual context for the author's words, a design that draws the reader into the book and conveys the reader effortlessly through the pages. The hand of the designer should be essentially invisible, no more than a ghostly beckoning to turn the page. As Claire points out, the best book designs are beautiful yet unnoticed by the reader; the best designs support the words without overwhelming them. You'll never be able to look at a book the same way again after reading her view of the unique art form known as book design.

With the completion of the copyediting and with the approval of the design specifications, the production editor, who reports to the managing editor, dispatches all the materials outside the house to the compositor, where the words and the design come together in the first stage of the production process.

Elyse Dubin, Sylvia Miller's mentor, wanted a job that combined words and art, and she found it in production at the scholarly and scientific publisher Pergamon Press. Often, smaller houses and nontrade publishers such as scientific, technical, and medical publishers hire smart people with little experience and allow them a great deal more independence than they would find as beginners at a large trade house. Elyse was able to plunge right into what she calls "the blood and guts of publishing. Production is where the whole raw mess begins and where the finished book is crafted." She was with Pergamon for three years before moving on to Macmillan, where she was eventually promoted to managing editor; she is now associate director of production for the adult trade division of HarperCollins Publishers. Elyse considers herself, as she has titled her essay, "Blessed and Cursed," simultaneously drawn to books and overwhelmed by the challenges of producing them, but always exhilarated by "publishing fever."

The last freelancer to be tapped by the production editor, the last person to work on the book before manufacture begins, is the indexer. For the first time in his professional life, Sydney Wolfe Cohen's work will not come last—at least his essay won't. In "Enter Indexer," Sydney eloquently describes a beginning indexer's life, just as he distills other people's writing when he provides concise, comprehensive, accessible indexes of their books. He provides the textual equivalent of a pointing index finger as he relates the story of how he became overtaken by the indexer's art.

Sydney tells us that no one actually intends to make a career of indexing; he considered it a stopgap producer of extra income until he could find a "real" publishing job in-house. Ironically, he became so successful as a freelancer that he took on staff to handle the press of work and now presides over his own "in-house" corporate culture. Sydney and his associates, some of whom were trained in the art of indexing in Sydney's class at NYU's School of Continuing Education, produce indexes for almost all the major houses and many other publishers as well. With the production of this orderly summation, the book is at last ready for manufacture—for the words and images to meet the paper, the press, and the binder.

While all the editors and editorial production people and designers and manufacturers are spending a lot of time and money making the book as good as it can be, the marketing groups are gearing up to figure out how to sell the book and bring in a few dollars to offset the huge bills being constantly incurred in this prepublication stage. The person who worries every day about every dollar from acquisition to the last copy sold is the chief financial officer. All CFOs in book publishing have a job that is stressful and challenging and absolutely crucial to the entire publishing operation. Before we proceed to meet the marketers who will present the finished book to the world, let's spend a few minutes looking over the shoulder of the person in charge of the checkbook.

Thomas S. Novak, now CFO of Beacon Press, a small Boston publisher, began his book publishing career as business manager for David R. Godine, Publisher, Inc., also a distinguished independent press based in Boston. In his essay, "What Is a Cash Cow, Anyway?" Tom describes how work that is difficult and demanding in any house becomes even more critical at a small press where there is no margin for error, no safety net. Though Tom learned to break the tension with a good joke from time to time, stress has always remained integral to his job. Small presses have got to be good to survive; it may be their sense of continual adventure that gives an edge to the better ones. Tom does a great job describing the working atmosphere in one of the country's most interesting independent presses while also surveying the sometimes peculiar financial issues of concern to all publishers from kitchentable operations to multinational conglomerates.

One of the first marketers who may be able to begin to bail out the beleaguered chief financial officer is the subsidiary rights director, who is frequently able to negotiate a license long before a book is ready to be published. There are many ways in which intellectual property may be exploited. Traditionally, books begin life in the hardcover format, though there are many paperback originals, both trade paperback and mass-market; hardcovers are often reprinted in paperback. Books can also be excerpted in magazines, offered as book club editions or as collections of condensed books, or as movies or stage shows or audiotapes. Books (and their various offspring) can appear translated into other languages. Subrights people try to exploit the book in as many ways as possible by licensing to other publishers and purveyors of other media the right to use the material in a certain form, in a certain geographical territory, for a certain time, at a good price, which is shared with the author.

In her essay, Kristin Kliemann, now the subsidiary rights director of Hyperion/Disney Press, declares herself "Willing to Be Lucky," and indeed she has been, stumbling somewhat haphazardly into her profession. When Kris started in the business, she was convinced that working in subrights was "the greatest job in publishing ever," and she still thinks so. The work is endlessly variable and allows a great deal of contact with publishing people outside your own house. And today subrights people find themselves in the vanguard of the electronic/digital revolution, continually imagining new ways of getting the word out. The electronic/

multimedia field is too new to be constrained by tradition or convention; any kind of deal is possible. Kris and her colleagues are literally defining and redefining their jobs every day. Subrights is evolving at a remarkably fast pace, and Kris's employers and authors (and her students at NYU) benefit from her ability to adapt quickly to the new and emerging markets.

Licensing subrights is a crucial step in bringing books to the marketplace. But when publishing people speak of "marketing," they're usually referring to advertising, sales promotion, and publicity. Maryann Palumbo is now vice president and director of marketing for the many mass-market paperback imprints of Penguin USA. Like many other people whose essays appear here, she started as a secretary, in her case assisting the vice president of sales at World Publishing Company. But she soon managed to change her clerical job into a successful publishing career simply by volunteering to help her colleagues when time allowed. In her essay, "Dancing School," Maryann makes the point that publishing is a team effort and that people need to work in sync with their colleagues in order to be effective. This is particularly true in marketing. For example, there's not much point in undertaking an expensive advertising campaign in San Francisco if most of the books (and the posters or other point-of-purchase promotional materials) have been shipped to East Coast bookstores while the author is scheduled to make media appearances in Chicago and Dallas. Coordinating sales promotion, author publicity, and advertising effectively is a great deal more difficult than you might think, an observation which is seconded by other essayists writing about their own work in publicity and sales. But when everyone is dancing together, tremendous numbers of books will find their way to eager readers; the author and the booksellers will be just as pleased as the publisher.

Getting the books into the stores is the job of the sales representatives, whose work begins long before publication when reps from all over the country convene at a sales conference with editors and marketers who describe the upcoming titles, show the jackets, and discuss the marketing plans. Then, armed with order forms and catalogs touting the new books, the sales reps hit the road to spread the good news to their accounts. Gregory Brandenburgh, now vice president of international sales for HarperCollins San Francisco, spent his first year in publishing as a rep for a small evangelical Christian publishing house called Fleming H. Revell. He reports in his essay, "Hey, Lady, Ya Wanna Buy a Book? *or* My First Year as a Traveling Book Salesman," that he drove over 50,000 miles that year, covering a territory that stretched from Fresno, California, north to the Canadian border and east to the Nebraska state line.

His "naive notions" of what he would experience in selling books to religious bookstores were quickly dispelled on his very first sales call, during which he came to understand a crucial lesson about booksellers and their concerns. What Greg learned throughout his first year of living on the front line of the book business are lessons that any sales rep anywhere marketing any kind of book would recognize as essential to effective selling.

Publicists, along with other marketers, plot their strategies months in advance of a book's publication and then send out early copies to certain key players in the media such as producers of nationally broadcast talk shows and influential book review editors. But the actual publicity doesn't hit the airwaves (or the print media) until books have arrived in the stores. William Parkhurst, now president of Parkhurst Communications, a media consulting firm specializing in training authors for radio and television appearances and in producing syndicated radio features for publishers, had an amazing first year in book publishing, as he relates in his story, "Champagne Corks and Mafia Killers." On his very first day on the job at Pocket Books, the mass-market imprint of Simon & Schuster, Bill, the only man in the publicity department, was expected to arrange a five-city author tour for Nancy Friday, who was promoting the paperback edition of her best-seller *My Secret Garden: Women's Sexual Fantasies.* Most new publicists begin with somewhat less provocative material but move up to mafia hit men and other notorious or notable authors fairly quickly.

A publicist's work is arguably even more important in promoting the books that are not expected to be best-sellers. The typically modest advertising budget allocated to these "midlist" books has to cover advertising to the trade as well as advertising to the consumer. Anything less than a major ad campaign may go virtually unnoticed by the consumers it is meant to influence. Publicity isn't free; publishers have to pay publicists' salaries or fees, as well as the cost of producing press releases, press kits (more elaborate packages), authors' photographs, advance reading copies (clean manuscripts or bound proofs), review copies of the finished books, postage, phone bills, authors' travel expenses, and so on. But a few favorable reviews in a few major metropolitan newspapers can be much more effective in selling the book than buying two or three times the advertising space; and if a publicist can convince a major talk show producer to showcase an author, success is almost guaranteed. While much of the marketing effort is aimed at getting the books *into* the bookstores (certainly a good starting point), publicists are most effective in getting the books *out* of the stores.

Books that sit too long on bookstore shelves end up in one of two places. Hardcovers and trade paperbacks are returned to the publishers' warehouses (and may or may not be shipped out for another try), whereas mass-market paperbacks end up in Dumpsters, their covers stripped off and returned for credit. Perhaps apocryphally, the publisher Alfred A. Knopf is cited as having commented on the subject of returned books, "Gone today; here tomorrow." One effective method booksellers have traditionally employed to avoid unsold stock is known as "hand-selling," a personal and often well-informed approach to a potential buyer. An extraordinary example of an attempt at hand-selling is featured in the account of Robert B. Wyatt, who spent his first two years in book publishing at Doubleday's flagship store on Fifth Avenue in New York City. Bob, who is now president of his own imprint, A Wyatt Book for St. Martin's Press, has entitled his essay "Ignorance and Curiosity" with good reason: both attributes have paid off handsomely for him in the long run. His experience as a bookseller, though somewhat different from that of the moonlighting Jane von Mehren, has given him a frontline perspective of the ultimate publishing activity, an understanding that is far too often lacking in the publishing professionals who deliver the book to the store.

Bookselling has changed a great deal in the last few years from the advent of national chains to their development of the so-called superstores, and few people in publishing doubt that bookselling will be changed further by the evolution of an electronic "information superhighway." But by the same token, there will always be readers who value the advice of a bookseller who knows both the books and the readers personally, who can take a book, hand it to a reader, and say, as Andre Schiffrin said to Joy Smith, "You might like this. It is very good." That, ultimately, is the object of book publishing.

If you're one of those people who sacrifice much needed sleep to read just one more chapter before turning out the light, if you interrupt your friends because you can't wait to tell them about a wonderful new writer you've discovered, if you begin to panic when your stack of new, unread books shrinks to a mere five feet, then it's time to acknowledge your obsessive behavior and join those of us who derive singular satisfaction from contributing to the process of making an author's words publicly available in the form of a book. By helping to provide entertainment and information, by offering new voices and new visions, you'll be nourishing our culture in a way that no one else can. And you'll be in the vanguard of the electronic revolution, armed with technology that will stretch the known limits of human communication and change our world forever. Welcome to book publishing!

1

Interested in a Career in Book Publishing?

GREGORY GIANGRANDE

Let education be a sort of amusement; you will then be better able to find out the natural bent.

—Plato

Education was definitely an amusement for me. I always felt school was a fun, interesting way to pass the time until I figured out my "natural bent." During my early years I was preoccupied with developing my baseball and basketball skills so I could play for the Yankees or the Knicks. Of course, it didn't occur to me then that what I enjoyed most in school—reading and writing—were interests around which I could develop a more realistic career.

At thirteen, discovering my "natural bent" suddenly became "what am I going to do with my life" angst. Doctor, lawyer, policeman, actor, singer, depending on which star or television series was popular at the time. I was sure of only one thing: I *needed* to do something fun and creative.

I say *needed* because, unless circumstances prevent you from doing otherwise, why not do something that you enjoy, that doesn't even seem like work? And if you're truly fortunate, why not do something that you would do even if you weren't getting paid?

That epiphany turned my angst to excitement. I loved words and information—written and spoken. I read everything—books, newspapers, magazines, and cereal boxes. I was moved not only by the written word but by the oral interpretation of written words. From the power and poetry of Martin Luther King, Jr.'s "I Have A Dream" speech to the masterful imagery of Hemingway, I knew then that words, whether to educate, enlighten, or entertain—spoken or written—were my "natural bent."

I firmly believe in the "pave the road as you go along" philosophy, but I also believe that you can't fight the driving force of fate. In the eighth grade I knew that I wanted to study journalism at New York University. The next four years were spent sailing along that route, becoming editor of my junior high school yearbook and later the editor of the high school newspaper. Sometime during my senior year at NYU I realized that although I was doing what I wanted to do, I still didn't know what I wanted to be when I grew up! Fate played a hand when I was offered a scholarship to pursue a master's degree in communications at NYU. I figured this was a perfect opportunity for me not only to delay growing up but to round out my fascination with words as well.

During grad school I met the owner of a floundering local newspaper in Brooklyn, New York. It was a cheap tabloid void of any redeeming social value. I casually commented that what the local area really needed was a community issues-oriented newspaper, something upbeat, useful, and relevant. Two months later I was running a 20,000-circulation weekly, which he financed. For the next two years I pursued my M.A. part-time and worked full-time, forty to fifty hours per week, nights, weekends, and loving every second of it. This wasn't work really; it was fun.

My book publishing career began at Random House, where I started as a college recruiter interviewing and talking to thousands of students across the country about the industry and what it takes to get a job and succeed in it. I traveled extensively, scouting for students with the greatest potential, raw talent, and passion that it takes to succeed in this business. Let me share with you some of the ideas I discussed with those college students in talk after talk throughout that first year and ever since.

Do you think publishing is your "natural bent"? That's one of the first questions I've asked those thousands of students from schools all over the country who after four years of college are contemplating which road to choose after graduation. The fundamental question you must ask yourselves is, Why book publishing?

Your answer will determine whether or not you embark on this path or take another. But let's keep the decision making in perspective. At this point in your life, choosing a career is like watching TV: You can surf through many channels and sample different programs. Eventually, something will excite you enough to make you want to settle down, explore, and savor—like curling up with a good book!

You love books. You feel sheepish about admitting it because it sounds trite, clichéd. However, if it is true, if you are thinking about a career in publishing because you do love books, then you're on the right track. The love, the passion for your work is the force that will propel and prepare you for the long haul of any career—especially one in publishing.

Let's explore this point further. You love books because of their ability to inform, influence, and enrich the culture. You are the kind of person who can't pass a bookstore without stopping to look at the window display, the kind who gets lost in a bookstore for an hour when you thought only ten minutes had passed. What may be more difficult or even embarrassing for you to admit is that books excite you in ways that may have had you concerned. I know I'm going to get some good-natured ribbing from my colleagues for writing the next sentences, but the fact is that only those people who have become jaded won't remember that they once felt this way, too. Even with all the recent and exciting technological advances, with books on CD-ROM and interactive media becoming part of the industry, you love the object itself, which has withstood centuries of technological achievement. The smell, look, and feel of books; cradling them in your hands, cracking the spine, turning the pages. Is this passion or perversion? Hopefully it's passion—a prerequisite for a successful career in any industry but especially one in book publishing. (If none of this resonates, there is always investment banking, insurance, pharmaceutical sales, and so on.)

Why is loving what you do so important? Because chances are, you'll spend more time working than doing anything else in your life! Think about it. The next forty years or so of your life will be spent working. Think about the classes you've taken in college. The ones you love seem to just fly by. The others—an eternity. Dragging yourself to class is as difficult as sitting through it. Imagine a job like that. Eight hours per day, every day, five days per week.

Publishing may very well be just like the best course you've ever taken: a stimulating environment where interesting, intelligent, creative individuals share their diverse talents and experiences while working with books. There aren't any tests, term papers, or grades—but you do get paid! Not much to start, though. While publishing is notorious for its low entry-level salaries, they have approached respectability in recent years. And it's a myth that one must take a vow of poverty for a lifetime. There really is no limit on how much you can earn or how high you can go. It's up to you. But it takes time and a lot more to make this happen. It takes initiative.

Typical entry-level job descriptions begin "individual will assist with various office duties including typing, filing, answering phones, xeroxing, etc." I know what you're thinking; I heard all about it from campus to campus. You didn't spend up to $100,000 on a college education to become a secretary. However, just being in the publishing environment as someone's assistant provides you with an opportunity to learn a tremendous amount by osmosis. Your chances of advancing to a higher position depend on whether you can see beyond the clerical work. The following literary analogy accurately reflects the common refrain of those most and least likely to succeed.

A TALE OF TWO ASSISTANTS

It Was the Best of Times

"The phone rang incessantly all morning; everybody wanted something. Agents, authors, production people, contracts people. I barely had time to make copies of that new manuscript. I think it's terrific, especially this latest draft. Things finally settled down enough in the afternoon for me to concentrate on writing the readers' reports for the manuscripts I read at home last weekend. Typed and filed some rejection letters—thought the comments by the editor were constructive."

It Was the Worst of Times

"I spent the entire day typing, filing, copying, and answering the phone. Maybe tomorrow I'll get to do a mailing."

Your first job in book publishing is what you make it. It's an apprenticeship, and there aren't any shortcuts. You start at the bottom, pay your dues, learn the trade, and make yourself so invaluable that you leave the company no choice but to promote you—or lose you to the competition. That's how your boss started, and your boss's boss. It's a highly competitive industry, but if you possess the two key ingredients essential for success— initiative and talent—book publishing offers several exciting and rewarding career opportunities.

A Tale of Two Assistants illustrated a day in the life of an editorial assistant. That's the job most students think of when considering a career in book publishing. But there's so much more. In fact, editorial accounts for only 15 percent of all the job opportunities in publishing. Some of the other 85 percent includes publicity, promotion, production, sales, marketing, subsidiary rights, contracts, and design, many of which you'll learn about in the ensuing chapters. Each plays an important and distinctive role in the publishing process, offering an array of career tracks to which you can closely match your own particular interests, skills, and abilities. So keep an open mind. Whichever you choose, you're working with books!

Discovering your niche is the easy part. Obtaining the opportunity to carve it out is somewhat more challenging. The competition for entry-level jobs can be fierce. Many of the larger well-known publishing houses routinely receive several hundred résumés per month, yet the entry-level jobs they need to fill may be only several dozen—per year! Although the odds aren't in your favor, there is a lot you can do to improve them considerably. The students with whom I spoke during my recruiting trips always asked for insider's tips on landing that first job.

If it's not too late, try to obtain an internship in the field before you graduate. The experience will be invaluable, not only in terms of what you'll learn but also because of whom you may meet. Publishing is a small industry, and networking is a big part of it. Interns who do well often get the inside track for full-time jobs when they become available. The internship also provides an opportunity to make contacts and utilize them for leads elsewhere. In general, you should contact everyone you know—friends, family, school alumni, et al.—who works in the industry or who may know someone else who does. Requesting just a few minutes of their time for an informational interview and following that up with a short, professional thank-you note can go a long way in getting your name and résumé around, so you'll be kept in mind when positions do become available.

At the very least, a publishing internship on your résumé will help set it apart from the résumés without one. And while we're on the subject, your résumés should be perfect. High-quality paper in any shade of white will do. If you think that a fuschia résumé will stand out from the pile—you're right—the color makes it easier to be transferred to the rejection pile! A résumé should be a professional presentation of yourself—typeset, free of errors, neat, clean, well-written, inviting to read, and ONE PAGE! This may be book publishing, but we're not interested in your autobiography. While all of this may seem obvious, you'd be surprised how many résumés don't satisfy even one of the criteria. With the huge volume of applicants, employers don't need many reasons to reject a résumé. Don't give them any!

However, even the most impressive résumé can't do more than get you an interview. *You* must be impressive in the interview to get the job. Four years of hard work and study can become irrelevant in the first four minutes of an interview if you haven't prepared properly. Do you look and act like employees in the organization who have positions similar to the one for which you are applying? Or do you look and act like a student—fraternity brother or sorority sister—dressing up for an interview? More-over, you must know the industry, the company, and the job. Know who you are, what you want, and why you want it. Avoid pat answers ("I'm a people person who likes to see projects through to completion") and questions that are inappropriate for the first interview ("What are the company benefits?").

The Career Development Center of your college can be a great resource. Your tuition helps pay for the center whose services may include mock interviewing sessions in which you can practice and obtain invaluable interviewing tips. The college career counselors also may conduct résumé-writing workshops, offer information about employers, and post listings for jobs and internships.

Although book publishing is not an academic discipline usually found in undergraduate college, there are several publishing pro-grams offered at universities around the country which are grow-ing in popularity. The most common are the Summer Publishing Institutes, four- to seven-week programs designed to give partici-pants an overview of the industry. Some are devoted exclusively to book publishing; others cover book and magazine publishing. The courses are taught by industry professionals and provide an oppor-tunity not only to learn about the various career paths but to network as well. While these programs can be helpful and usually have high rates of placement, they can also be costly (anywhere from $2,000 to $4,500 depending on the program) and are by no means necessary for getting a job.

Aside from these special programs, I'm often asked what course of college study is appropriate for a career in book publishing. You need go no farther than the nearest bookstore for the answer. The breadth and quantity of topics and titles published under-score the importance of a well-rounded education, an education that crosses the boundaries of one particular course of study.

Many enter the profession full of idealism, embracing the romantic notion of literature and publishing as a noble endeavor. While the profession is respectable, it is also very much a business, a fun, exciting, creative business dedicated to earning a profit through publishing books. Learning the fundamental principles of accounting, finance, economics, and marketing is as important as a concentration in the humanities.

If Plato is right, whatever you study is "a sort of amusement" so that you may be "better able to find out the natural bent." For me, book publishing has been an exciting journey of exploring, learning, and growing. I still don't know what I want to be when I grow up, but I do believe I've discovered my "natural bent."

Gregory Giangrande is the manager of human resources at Random House and an adjunct instructor of communications at New York University.

2

Take the Book!

 L A U R A J . B L A K E

A writer friend of mine had been trying to get an agent for his fiction for several years. Having been thoroughly rejected by almost every agent in the business, he painted a very dark picture of the book agent—a despicable parasite who fed off the blood and sweat of undoubtedly talented, tireless artistic souls, contributing precious little to the creative process, suppressing the creative efforts of many writers (meaning my friend) by not embracing the undiscovered genius of those toiling away at their Great American Novels. His view, of course, was a tad biased. Despite his antipathy, the idea of being a literary agent intrigued me, and so I did some research.

I had little idea of what the job itself entailed except that literary agents often did seem to hold the key to fame and fortune for many aspiring writers. I also held the romantic view that the literary agent read novels for a living, and as an English major, that sounded pretty good to me. I wrote letters to about a dozen of the larger New York agencies asking if they would be kind enough to spare a few moments of their time to sit down and describe to me exactly what they did to earn their keep. I got one letter back. Perry Knowlton, chairman and CEO of Curtis Brown, Ltd., was the only one to respond to my request. Since that summer eight years ago, he has been very generous with his support of me as a developing young agent, as has Peter Ginsberg, president of Curtis Brown, Ltd., whose patience and guidance have been invaluable.

I worked as an intern at Curtis Brown that first summer, filling in for vacationing assistants, sorting through piles of unsolicited mail from hopeful writers, reading manuscripts for agents whose reading load made their offices seem like fire hazards. The sinister specter of the book agent as a ruthless shark, feeding off the creative juices of innocent writers was nowhere to be found. As it turned out, by the end of that summer I saw both agent and author quite differently than when I'd arrived three months earlier.

Although I suppose it's possible to characterize a literary agent as a parasite, my experience indicates that an author with an agent will often make more money than one without. Retaining the services of a reputable agent will ensure that an author's publishing rights have been well protected. Agents, I learned, play many roles. I saw book agents in the role of therapist as well as accountant; confidant as well as editorial adviser; tough-talking negotiator as well as smooth-talking diplomat; tolerant listener as well as tireless advocate. I began to see authors as a rather haphazard collection of diligent, quirky, demanding, unpredictable, sometimes unstable individuals whose creative efforts frequently need guidance and protection. Now *there* was a challenge. Though the world of publishing has changed dramatically since my days as a summer intern, my general view of the roles of author, agent, and publisher has remained more or less constant ever since.

After my graduation from Vassar, I began to work full-time at Curtis Brown as an assistant to a young agent, Henry Dunow.

From the start it was a good match. We shared a similar taste in books, and he was good enough to solicit my opinion on the various projects he was considering to represent. There wasn't anything he wouldn't do for his clients—their needs became his own. To this day I don't know any other agent who handles his writers with more tolerance and indulgence. There's no doubt that some of that has rubbed off on me, in the approach I take to my own clients, though it can be very dangerous to overindulge creative writers. They tend to call you up at all hours of the day or night when they're hit with a sudden attack of writer's block. I learned early that it's important to set limits (or at least to keep your home phone number to yourself).

James Oliver Brown, one of the most respected and most prominent agents in the business, had retired from Curtis Brown several years before I arrived, but his distinguished approach to his clients and to the profession in general still lingers in the books that line the halls of the Curtis Brown offices. Part of my responsibility was to look after his former clients, which meant renewing copyrights in their work, granting permission to others to quote from their material, and occasionally licensing a book to be reprinted. It was not altogether exciting stuff, but in having access to his clients, their files, their correspondence, and of course their work, I learned important things from a great agent I barely knew and rarely saw. His graceful demeanor and exceedingly honorable approach to his profession made a very distinct impression. He wrote once that he would never represent someone whom he wasn't able to call his friend. Securing a huge advance was not the primary motivation for Mr. Brown. The quality of the individual was as important to him as the quality of the material. These days it's a rare agent who can follow this tack, but it has always provided a model to keep in mind.

As the youngest agent at Curtis Brown, my boss Henry was

responsible for the unsolicited letters, manuscripts, and phone calls from the steady stream of writers in need of representation, all of them convinced their books would become the next all-time best-selling headline-grabbing blockbusters. Every now and then we'd find a talented writer with a good story to tell (a combination that's a bit more rare than you'd expect) in the "slush pile," but the majority of the inquiries to our office were not fruitful. I got a kick out of the letters, all too many of which began, "I am presently incarcerated in the state correctional facility at Hudson, New York. . . . I have written a 100,000 word novel entitled *Bad Dreams* which tells the story of one man's personal struggle to keep his genetically altered brain from destroying himself and those around him." There is a constant supply of letters from those claiming to be Jesus Christ, the daughter of Marilyn Monroe, or inhabited by an alien from another planet.

Then there was the odd client who refused to sign her book contract because Mercury was in retrograde. The mystery writer who became so obsessed with the sleuth in her series of mysteries that she began to dress like, sound like, and generally behave like her main character. She even once signed her contract as her sleuth.

No day with creative writers is ever the same.

I must admit that my first year in publishing I spent a great deal of time answering the phone, typing letters, and drinking lots of tea. I made plenty of elementary mistakes, even with the limited responsibility that I was given. The sheer volume of printed material coming in and going out of the office is tremendous, and inevitably every now and then a manuscript meant for Editor A at Publisher B would end up on the desk of Editor Y at Publisher Z. It's 10:00 A.M., do you know where your submissions are?

One morning our receptionist rang my desk, obviously very upset, asking that someone (meaning me) be kind enough to speak with a very determined, completely certifiable nutcase who refused to leave without giving her manuscript to a qualified member of the firm for a thorough evaluation. Unsuspecting as I was, I strolled confidently out to the reception area intending to educate another eager yet well-meaning writer about the proper way to approach an agent.

"I've found the Fountain of Youth," she began.

"Where?" I asked, feeling smug. She was no spring chicken, I noticed, so whatever it was she'd found, she could have used a few more hits.

"It's all in my book." With that she held out the manuscript. I put my hands in my pockets.

"We don't read unsolicited manuscripts," I told her, with charm to spare. "Write a letter describing your book and enclose a self-addressed stamped envelope. We'll read your letter and let you know if we're interested in taking a look."

"No, I don't think so." She took a deliberate step toward me. Her body was shaking; either she was older than I thought, or she was about to let me have it. It was about this time I realized that this was no ordinary desk job. This was exciting, even dangerous. Special Agent Laura Blake.

"I came all the way from Staten Island. Take the book." She shoved the manuscript into my stomach. *"Take the book!"* She was stronger than she looked. Maybe she'd found that fountain after all. Or perhaps she was pumped up from hauling her tome all over town. So I did what every inexperienced, well-behaved, intimidated twenty-one-year-old would do. I took the book. We sent it back a few days later, but the experience taught me a valuable lesson—always take the book from a disturbed maniac. The reception area is no place to be a hero.

Learning about the publishing of books is an ongoing process. No other industry produces tens of thousands of entirely new products each year the way publishers do. The book business absorbs and reflects the ever-changing issues and trends in American culture—from food to flower-gardening; from sex to science; from perfume to politics—and you can get a good sense of what's on the mind of Americans by thumbing through a publisher's catalog. Since writers need agents before many publishers will consider their material, agents are often the first to glimpse the next change in the current of American society, and publishers rely on us to bring it to their doors. It's a system of reliance that more often than not works very well.

Since my days as a summer intern at Curtis Brown, more than eight years ago, I've learned a lot about how to be an effective agent, but there's always more to be learned. Knowing when to fight and when to back off, being able to gauge sensitive writers' emotional needs and when to nag them to get their work done, knowing when to listen and when to come down hard—it's clear to me that this is a craft like any other, involving skills that need constant honing and refining. I'd recommend it to anyone who likes to fight for the little guy, can appreciate the creative process, and has an eye for a good book.

Laura J. Blake represents a wide range of fiction, nonfiction, and children's book authors as an agent at Curtis Brown, Ltd., where she has worked for over eight years.

3

Of Filing Cabinets and Publishers' Invoices

 JANE VON MEHREN

On my first day in publishing I was worried about arriving at my new office too early. Several weeks earlier I had been hired as an editorial assistant by James O'Shea Wade, then a senior editor at Crown Publishers, Inc. At the end of my junior year at Vassar College—being only a thesis away from graduation—I decided to enter the "real world." I had decided on publishing because it would allow me to work with the written word without having to undergo the anxiety of facing the blank page or the agonies of creation. So I called everyone I knew in publishing and combed the "Help Wanted" ads in the *New York Times*. After numerous interviews, I was offered a job by an academic press and by Crown; I accepted Crown's offer because I wanted to work with books that I might read, as opposed to scholarly tomes that I probably would not. And that first morning I was so excited I woke as soon as it was light out, and though I tried to delay myself I ended up

For James O'Shea Wade: mentor, teacher, friend, and editor extraordinaire.

on the subway realizing that since the masses of people on the train didn't actually slow it down, I was in danger of arriving much earlier than 9:30 when I was expected. So I exited the subway before my stop and walked the rest of the way.

I still arrived too early.

As I awaited my new boss, I looked around the cubicle that I would be sharing with a desk, a chair, a typing table that held one of the most ancient typewriters I had ever seen, a phone, In and Out baskets, and two filing cabinets. On the wall were several shelves filled with books, beneath which stood one of the filing cabinets on which a pile of multicolored manuscript boxes was stacked. It could only be described as small and very cramped, but it was all mine and I was thrilled.

Soon after, Jim arrived. A man who believes that you learn by doing, he got me started right away. We talked a bit about *Nop's Trials*, a heartwarming novel by Donald McCaig, in the tradition of James Herriot's novels, which he had given me during my interview and which had just been published; then he began telling me about the titles that were in the throes of production or still being written. Jim suggested that I begin by trying to get through the filing that had piled up in the absence of an assistant; in the process I could read through the files and see what I could learn.

I set to work on the humongous pile of paper that had been left behind by the former assistant, who, bless her heart, clearly wanted me to learn all about those files! I opened one drawer, then another, and then a third. As I began to shove papers in, the entire cabinet began to tilt in my direction! There I was: twenty-one years old, five feet, one inch tall, with a massive filing cabinet rushing toward me, about to have a very short publishing career. Embarrassed and scared, I tried to hold the cabinet up, when behind me I heard, "*Jane*, Oh my *Lord*," as Jim ran out to rescue me.

Within the first three hours on the job, I had learned a cardinal rule: Open only one file drawer at a time. The files were a source of a great many other lessons, as I discovered when I read through them during those early weeks. First, I was able to figure out who people were: were they authors, agents, foreign publishers, colleagues from other departments, or writers Jim was hoping to commission to write books at some future point in time? But even more important was what I gleaned about who my new boss was and what kind of editor he was and is. Through the enormous records Jim kept—nothing was ever thrown out—I began to see that being an editor is about taking care of your authors, their words, and their books throughout the publishing process from contract through the dreaded remainder letter and beyond. His long and detailed editorial notes and letters were no less thorough than his memos to the art department making sure that the design of the book was to the author's liking and to the book's best advantage. He made sure that the catalog copy was acceptable to the author as well as the sales and marketing department and that we had records of all the discussions he had with an agent about a contract. I quickly realized what it is to be a hands-on editor: It means that you are always pushing your authors to write the best books they can, always pushing your colleagues to publish those books as successfully and as well as the publishing house is capable.

Because I sat in a cubicle right outside Jim's office, I also learned a great deal from listening to him on the phone—which rang constantly. As I overheard his calls I realized that an editor is many things to many people: a negotiator, a confidant and friend, a behind-the-scenes cheerleader, a troubleshooter, and a salesperson. Being an editor requires tremendous patience, tact, persuasiveness, and empathy. You need to persuade your colleagues to support you in a potential acquisition, to convince an agent that the terms you are offering for a particular book are the best possible for the book and its author, to cajole your authors to continue to work on manuscripts they want to be finished with, to elucidate your vision for how a book ought to be packaged to the art and design team, and to convince your salespeople to position your authors' books as aggressively as you feel they merit.

I began reading manuscripts. When Jim first asked me to take a look at a project, I was quite apprehensive. How was I to know what was publishable? When he explained that there are no hard-and-fast rules in acquiring books for the trade market, I was no more at ease. "It's all a matter of personal taste," he assured me. I secretly wondered whether my taste would be at all compatible with his; he tended toward cop novels, military history, and serious nonfiction, and I had just spent three years studying eighteenth- and nineteenth-century poetry. I quickly figured out that it isn't that hard to separate the wheat from the chaff; the fact is that most editors reject about ninety-nine percent of the manuscripts they receive. Because so much of what I read in those early months seemed dreadful to me, I became very excited when I read a novel that engaged me from beginning to end. I wrote a three-page, single-spaced report about the plot, the writing, and my enthusiasm. I was sure that this would be the first book that Jim would acquire on my recommendation. It didn't happen that way: Jim did affirm my sense that this was a better novel than most that we saw, but also pointed out that it was plagued by too much exposition. After reading so much truly terrible writing, it is sometimes tempting to see passable work as being much better than it is. That first year I spent hours reading all different kinds of manuscripts and proposals, sometimes at the office, but most often at home in the evenings or on the weekends. Not having a television, I had one less distraction to keep me from the manuscript pile that *never* disappeared.

The In and Out boxes that I had been so excited about on my

first day turned out to be the mail drop for Jim's and my office. Early in my tenure, I came across a large piece of cardboard with all kinds of art and copy glued on it lying on top of our In box. This was a jacket mechanical, which along with every other element of the book's progress through the production process eventually would arrive in our In box. Jim's and my responsibility was to check that the production and design departments had produced the physical book in a manner that reflected both the author's and the editor's intentions. Some materials generated during this process—such as the copyedited manuscript and the page proofs—would be sent to the author for approval. But often, it was up to Jim and me to check and recheck the flap copy or the front matter of a book to make sure that everything was as it should be. On one occasion we had printed but not yet bound a book before we noticed that (despite having looked at the front matter at least a dozen times before) the author's name was missing from the title page. Some mistakes you can ignore; this one we could not, and we had to reprint 35,000 copies of the book's first thirty-two pages!

In college, I had imagined that my future career would have me sitting in a rather dusty office surrounded by piles of manuscripts, which I would read and decide to acquire or decline. Then I would help each author turn the pile of pages into a masterpiece. But I quickly learned that this fantasy had only a little bit to do with the real world: The most important thing an editor can do for his or her authors is to make sure that their books are successful, financially successful. Both your job and the author's depend on the books making money. An editor who acquires books that consistently lose money for the company will be fired; an author who writes books that fail to make money for the company will not receive another contract from the editor and publisher.

During this first year, I was utterly surprised by the enormous responsibility editors have for shaping the way a publishing house looks at a book: how the staff will pitch it, position it, and sell it to bookstores. This means that an editor must be able to talk with publicists, salespeople, and booksellers alike—to understand their perspectives and to help them see how each book can be exploited for their needs.

At about the same time that I was trying to learn how an editor fashions this sales pitch, I was offered a part-time job at the Traveller's Bookstore; the store needed a bookkeeper, and I could come to work after my day at Crown. I jumped at the opportunity; I needed the money—publishing salaries are notoriously low—and I thought it might help me understand more about this perplexing role of salesperson I was going to have to play if I remained on the editorial side of publishing. During my evenings at the store, I learned a lot about bookselling, particularly as it is done by a carriage-trade store, as publishers call independent bookstores that cater to an upscale clientele. The people who worked at the Traveller's Bookstore knew a great deal about the books they sold and about travel in general; they advised their customers about everything from which books suited their budgets to which time of the year is best for travel to Nepal or Miami Beach. It confirmed my belief that what's inside the cover of a book does count: A *Michelin* guide is first-rate for those interested in all aspects of a place, whereas others might prefer a *Karen Brown's Country Inn* guide because they want to relax in the countryside. I also saw how influential a good bookstore clerk can be in selling lots of copies of a title if he or she is particularly excited by the book.

At that point in my career, I hadn't thought a great deal about how everyone makes money: the author, the bookstore, and the publisher. And this was what I really began to understand as I sat in the store's back room, preparing weekly deposits and paying bills. This was no easy matter since publishers' invoices are about as decipherable as their royalty statements—both require a measure of stamina to figure out how the computer came up with the final amount due (or in the author's case, how much of the advance remains unearned). But after several months a coherent picture began to emerge. Take a $20 hardcover book, for example. The bookstore pays the publisher approximately $10.80 for the book, keeping roughly $9.20 in revenues. From that revenue the store still has to pay for rent, electricity, salaries, shopping bags, and other overhead costs. Although it may seem that the publisher is doing better than the store in receiving $10.80 for the book, the publisher's costs are high as well. After paying the author $2.00 to $3.00 in royalties, the publisher is left with $7.80 to $8.80 to cover salaries; overhead; advertising, marketing, and publicity budgets; jacket art; as well as paper, printing, and binding costs. The author receives a royalty only after the advance has been earned out, which means that many authors never earn any money in addition to what the publisher initially paid them for the book. It quickly became clear that while a lot of money may be changing hands, making a great deal of money is not easy for publishers, booksellers, or most authors.

You may ask why any of us would remain in this business since clearly we're not in it for the money. But by the end of my first year I knew that I probably will never leave publishing. It is an industry full of smart, creative people who are all working together to produce books that are important in many ways: sometimes they are utilitarian, other times amusing, and often awe-inspiring. This is a business made up of former bookworms who spent their childhoods buried in books because the words they found there were the best entertainment and the characters the best friends they could ever have. And now as adults, they can relish working with like-minded people who share the mission of giving others that same experience—and maybe even making a little money too!

Jane von Mehren is the executive editor of Penguin Books; she also teaches at New York University's Center for Publishing. In 1989 she received the Tony Godwin Memorial Award, which recognizes youthful editorial excellence, and in 1993 she, along with thirty other editors from around the world, was chosen to attend the Jerusalem Book Fair as an editorial fellow.

4

I Didn't Get a Degree from Berkeley for This!

 K I M B E R L Y   W I A R

When a college friend who was working at the University of Chicago Press called to say the director of the press needed a secretary and encouraged me to apply, I was intrigued. I loved books, and I loved being in a university environment—my years as an undergraduate at the University of California, Berkeley, in the 1960s were exciting and intellectually stimulating. What could be better than a university press?

But move to Chicago? It meant moving, period. The press wasn't going to fly a secretary there for an interview, and I couldn't afford the trip just to interview. I almost passed it up, but my friend persuaded me to fly to Chicago and move in with her and her husband. I interviewed for the secretarial job and was hired. Morris Philipson was then and still is the director. A Columbia Ph.D. and published author, he might have intimidated me, but he didn't because he has a great sense of humor. We hit it off immediately. He also had (and continues to have) a reputation for treating his secretaries well, and I have had only two successors in the twenty-two years since I was promoted to assistant editor.

I had said in my interview I wanted to be an editor, without really knowing what editorial acquisitions entailed. He had replied that he was willing to allow me to read manuscripts for the editors and write reports. If I proved I could evaluate manuscripts, and then *if* an editor left, he would be willing to consider me for an assistant editor's position.

My primary responsibilities initially were, of course, typing, copying, filing, scheduling appointments, screening calls, and making travel arrangements. This was a learning experience in itself. I had never been a secretary. Morris used a dictaphone. Sometimes he liked to dictate in person. I had never seen a dictaphone and didn't take shorthand. Fortunately, the learning curve was brief. It took about five minutes to master the dictaphone, and I soon discovered that, as promised, he dictated slowly.

Morris wrote great letters to some very interesting people, so the correspondence was never boring. I learned how to write business letters—not that I wrote them, but I learned just by typing his.

Everything came through his office, so I got an invaluable overview of publishing and how the process works. Morris was also willing to explain—what makes a good trade jacket, for example. I remember he came out of his office one day and said, "What do you think of this jacket?" I thought it was great. He told me it wasn't a good trade jacket because the prospective title was unreadable at fifteen feet. The prospective buyer in a bookstore needed to be able to spot a desired title from a distance, he explained. I became familiar with the typefaces we used most often, learned what a form was, and came to realize that after a manuscript had been edited, the next step was to design it. Then galleys arrived, followed by page proofs and folded and gathered sheets. Somewhere along in here the mock-up and then the "blueline" for the jacket appeared, followed by the actual jacket. And finally the finished book.

Yet the excitement of being in publishing at a great press wore a bit thin in the tediousness of copying packets for the Board of University Publications committee meetings. Why does publishing generate so much paper? There was always the typing, the filing, and the telephones. My friend and I used to mutter, "I didn't get a degree from Berkeley for this!"

But what exhilaration when, true to his word, Morris asked me to read and evaluate a manuscript. I hoped it wasn't something like *Proto-Indian European Trees*, which Morris had described as a typical university press book when I first joined the press. (I thought it was about trees.) My heart sank when the manuscript turned out to be a children's book. As we didn't publish children's books, I inquired if we were seriously considering it and learned I had just asked the second question every editor must ask: Does it fit the list? The first, of course, is whether the manuscript is publishable. Morris replied that it wasn't likely we would take on a children's title but that the press was considering it. He assured me I should give the work serious consideration. I did my best and ended up recommending against publication. Soon I had another manuscript to evaluate. I learned a key lesson from this experience: to trust my instincts.

One of the most memorable things about my first year was the friends I made. Penny Kaiserlian, now associate director at the University of Chicago Press, was then the marketing manager's secretary. Henry Tom, currently executive editor at Johns Hopkins University Press, was the editor-in-chief's editorial assistant. Michael Denneny, senior editor at St. Martin's Press, was the senior editor's editorial assistant. And Marlie Wasserman, social sciences editor at Routledge, was the secretary to the social science editor. In various groupings we used to talk or have lunch and compare the worm's-eye view of how things worked at the press. I learned how valuable colleagues could be. That was in 1970, and we remain in touch today.

Terror struck when it came time for more formal social events, an integral part of publishing at Chicago. Morris loved to entertain. I couldn't make small talk and felt uncomfortable in large social groups. I remember being very intimidated at the first Laing Prize party to celebrate the publication of the book by a faculty member that had brought the greatest distinction to the press's list. At some point I must have told Morris something about how uncomfortable I felt making small talk because I remember he said, "Ah, but you're such a good listener." I didn't know that about myself. Over the years I have discovered that listening is a real asset to an acquisitions editor. I don't learn nearly as much by talking as I do by listening.

As the director's secretary, I interacted with all members of the book division staff, in editorial, marketing, and production, about seventy-five people. From these encounters I learned many things, such as the difference between copyediting and copywriting, and about trade and short discounts. I especially remember learning about the components of marketing—publicity, promotion, advertising, direct mail, and sales—and how different strategies worked depending on the discount, for example, that direct mail was essential for short-discount books.

There was also a journals division, so I became acquainted with the journals manager and some key staff. Our business office and warehouse, where at least 125 people worked, remained a mystery until I finally took a tour and was astounded to see the incredible inventory stacked to the very high ceiling. I did of course interact with the business manager and other staff on the telephone. Because of all this interaction, I gained confidence in dealing with people.

But always, there was the typing, the filing, the telephones.

Partway through my first year, it was announced that the press would be moving to new quarters. At the time the press occupied a wonderful red brick building with a copper roof. It was across the street from the uninspired administration building. Now the press would be relocating to the third and fourth floors of the administration building—a move that was not greeted with enthusiasm, even though it would give us more space. Morris's attitude was that the new location afforded the opportunity to look at the beautiful old press building or the quadrangle—much better views.

I was somewhat involved in the move, coordinating the efforts of our departments with the space coordinator from the university. I remember Morris cautioned me that some people—even those who seemed easygoing—would be difficult to work with because any change was threatening. I guess I hadn't realized that. As an army brat, I took change for granted. But he was right, for there was talk about who would have a window office and whether the view was of the quadrangle or the press building. I learned something about human nature that has served me well in dealing with authors.

Finally, I learned Morris's perspective on acquisitions. He believed in allowing an editor to pursue his or her interests within certain broadly defined areas. In doing so over time, a coherent list evolves.

Looking back, I perhaps appreciate more now how much I learned as secretary to the director. Although the bulk of my work was secretarial, every day brought contact with other members of the staff, as well as with authors, prospective authors, and staff at other publishing houses. Publishing was even more interesting than I had imagined, I guess because of all the details that did require attention. I remember a quote on Morris's wall that read something like this: "Publishing consists of hundreds of details, none of which are important unless omitted or done incorrectly."

Kimberly Wiar was promoted to acquisitions editor at the University of Chicago Press in 1971. Currently she is acquisitions editor with the University of Oklahoma Press, where she helped establish the American Indian Literature and Critical Studies Series. She acquires titles across a broad range of disciplines from humanities to science.

5

The Accidental Profession

 A N D R E A   C A S C A R D I

I've heard people say that publishing is "the accidental profession," and I guess in some ways that was true in my case. I didn't always know that I wanted to be an editor—in fact, I'm sure I didn't know that such a career even existed until I graduated from Holy Cross! I thought that I might like to write for a magazine, however, and I thought that I ought to know something about how magazines worked before I went to them and asked for a job. So I applied to several postgraduation summer programs in publishing and chose to attend the University of Denver Publishing Institute. One of the staff members was nice enough to give me a call and tell me the program didn't have anything to do with magazine publishing, only book publishing. I decided that was okay anyway, since I'd never been to Colorado and thought a summer in Denver would be interesting. Little did I know it would shape my entire future!

In Denver I met many smart, funny, excited people who held all sorts of interesting jobs in book publishing: subsidiary rights director, marketing director, editor-in-chief. These people got to read books and work with writers all day long. What a great way to make a living! But of all the positions I learned about, the one that I thought sounded best would be marketing children's books. After all, I reasoned, I loved literature as an adult because I'd loved reading as a child. There were books I'd read hundreds of times; I can still recite the opening lines of some of them. You really can't influence adults the way you can children, whose whole lives can be transformed by something they read. Wouldn't it be great to be someone who promoted children's books to the world—to get kids as excited about reading as I'd been?

So I returned from Denver to New York determined to find a job in children's book marketing, and I was lucky enough to be interviewed for such a position almost immediately. After an interview and a writing assignment (to write flap copy for two already published children's books), I was hired to be the promotion assistant at Charles Scribner's Sons in the children's book department.

My intellectual daydreams about the good I'd do in such a position were nearly immediately and quite thoroughly dashed. The reality of a promotion assistant's job day-to-day was quite different from what I'd imagined. I spent literally hours stuffing envelopes, updating charts of which books had been reviewed where (and making corresponding index cards), as well as all the typing, filing, and answering telephones I had expected. The hardest thing to discover about a disappointing first job is whether the problem is with you or with the job. Was I just not used to working full-time? Or was I really not meant to be a children's book marketer? I struggled with that question for several months until I decided I'd probably never know and that I should try something else.

I moved to Boston, where I had friends, and took the tougher road toward finding a job in a much smaller publishing community. I still believed publishing was the place for me, and I had complete certainty that I'd find the kind of *real* publishing job that fit my personality. No toy companies or even textbook publishers for me (as employment agencies tried to suggest)—I wanted trade, and I wanted children's books.

Again, luck was with me. I interviewed for a job in Houghton Mifflin's children's trade department. The editor-in-chief's secretary had died a year earlier and had never been replaced. I suppose I knew enough with my prior three months in promotion to give me the edge over candidates who were fresh out of school, but I didn't know so much that I'd be overqualified for the position. I was hired.

That year—my first as an editorial assistant—was when I really started my publishing career. After a year at Houghton Mifflin I think I finally understood why I was not as well suited to marketing as I was to editorial work. As an assistant to the editor-in-chief, I knew everything that was happening with every book from the moment it was submitted as a manuscript. I liked that especially and discovered as a result that I am very much an idea person. I think that your first working experience, no matter what it is, can be a period of self-discovery, and I was learning things about myself all the time.

I also learned the publishing process from beginning to end—not from some point halfway in between after the book has already been signed up and the manuscript delivered. That may be fine for some people, but I was pleased that my position enabled me to be in on the book from the very beginning, from the time the manuscript was first read or the art director first asked the artist to illustrate the book. When I read a manuscript, I could give my opinion about whether or not I thought an editor should give it a second reading—that is, my opinion counted for something in the potential life of a book. There was nothing more exciting than finding a "possible" in the pile of manuscripts that mostly would be returned with "form decline" letters. I learned, too, that most of those "possible" manuscripts don't make it onto the publishers' lists, perhaps one of the most important lessons of the first year. An editor or an editorial assistant needs to be able to see a germ of potential in a manuscript and encourage a writer to develop that germ, but it is the writer who must take it the next step. I discovered through many months of correspondence with writers who had a good idea but who couldn't develop it effectively just how difficult it is to be a successful writer.

And I learned how one approaches an author or illustrator about the work they have submitted. As I typed countless letters, I found out, for example, how to let an author know what you like about his or her work and still point out what could be improved. To this day, I still find myself calling up phrases from the past that are especially apt for this purpose. There is an editorial way of thinking that you can't ever study; the closest you can come to studying it is to work for a really talented editor, as I did, and absorb everything you can from that individual.

I learned a great deal about children's book publishing that year: why reviews are important in the life of a children's book; what a backlist is; what "blues" and "f and g's" are; what comprises front matter. There are many, many details to keep track of. You must be a sponge and must ask questions constantly to understand completely all the little bits and pieces that go into making a book, because eventually you'll be responsible for seeing that all those little bits and pieces end up in the right place in the book at the right time.

Being an acquisitions editor means having the "big picture," especially in children's books. Although children are the ultimate consumers of books, they are not the buyers—adults are. So a children's book editor has to understand what works with children and also what works with adults. The best authors and illustrators are the ones who call up the child inside themselves when they are creating their work. That's what an editor has to do, as well—always read with the child in you in mind.

In hindsight, I am so very glad that I was unhappy enough to leave my first job after only three months, because otherwise I might never have discovered how wonderful it is to be a children's book editor.

Andrea Cascardi, currently associate publisher at Hyperion Books for Children, is also the author of Good Books to Grow On: A Guide to Building Your Child's Library from Birth to Age Five *(Warner Books).*

6

"You Might Like This; It Is Very Good"

 J O Y S M I T H

In my junior year in college, like many students I experienced an identity crisis, and career confusion, of course, followed. I was attending the University of Washington, majoring in psychology, with every intention of making the world feel better through my future practice as a therapist. But I became less and less attracted to a profession spent listening to other people's problems. I discovered that counselor positions were few and hard to get, and I knew that social workers and therapists required an advanced degree in order to practice. I also knew that I did not want to attend graduate school any time in the near future. The search for another career was on.

Since my interests were mainly reading and writing, and I had long been aware of the fact that my grade point average was higher in literature courses than in psychology, I hoped to find a career that would suit these interests. Magazines and books seemed the obvious choice. At the university's career center I researched both fields but found little information except for a few short paragraphs here and there in reference books about media jobs. These tended to emphasize editorial positions in magazines. I spoke to a career counselor who described publishing as a "glamorous industry" with a history of family ownership employing upper middle-class, refined young men and women. She told me that it was also a low-paying, labor-intensive career. Her concluding words were that the few people she knew who had tried it did not last very long. These words would reverberate in my mind for years to come, a warning about the high turnover rate for young people in the industry—I think the saying is, "Publishing tends to eat its young."

During my senior year at the University of Washington, I was accepted into the Radcliffe Publishing Procedures course in Cambridge. My objective in applying for the course was to get to the East Coast, take a crash course in book and magazine publishing, and make contacts within the industry. At Radcliffe I found, as the career counselor had predicted, that I was surrounded for the most part by Ivy League– and Seven Sisters–educated people. As an African-American woman from a working-class background raised and schooled to enter into the white-collar world of the middle class, I decided publishing and the media in general were far too important and influential in our culture to be dominated by just one class and type of people. Now highly motivated, I felt that challenging the demographics of the business was another good reason to commit myself to publishing, at least for a while, if not for the long haul.

In 1987 the atmosphere that prevailed at the Radcliffe Publishing Procedures course was intense. There was so much material packed into this six-week course that the work actually began before you arrived. Radcliffe sent extensive homework assignments to the accepted college seniors during the madness of finals and graduation. Assignments were to be returned to Radcliffe before or upon arrival. Classes were scheduled back-to-back every day and evening. In addition to this rigorous schedule, there were two incredible, almost surreal, weeks when the participants were separated into groups and given the task of creating miniature book-publishing houses, and later in the summer, magazines. During this period each of us enacted jobs that mirrored a position within the publishing field with the requisite responsibilities. I hear it's less of a problem now, but in 1987 when I attended, the combination of stress and sleep deprivation did not make for an ideal situation. People well established in the publishing industry acted as consultants, but in the haze of creating magazines and publishing houses, it seemed nothing could alleviate our confusion. Somehow, though, by week's end we all completed our assignments.

At times Radcliffe participants socialized with publishing personalities who taught classes, attended late afternoon socials, and occasionally joined us for lunches or dinners. It was a great opportunity to make contacts, and some people were lucky enough to find jobs just from connections made at the course. Radcliffe provided me with a valuable network of friends whom I embraced and needed my first hectic and lonely year in New York. I also made contacts with established people, some of whom were helpful in my job search. Graydon Carter, now editor-in-chief of *Vanity Fair*, then editor-in-chief of *Spy Magazine*, was very generous with his time and advice. I think for those whose homes are not in the Northeast, the transition can be made much easier if you attend a summer publishing course. Scholarships are available.

The most important things I learned at Radcliffe were the daily goings-on in publishing and the many employment options within the book and magazine industry. In addition to the editorial department, there are career opportunities in publicity, advertising, sales, marketing, and production.

Contrary to popular belief, entry-level jobs in publishing do exist. For a paltry salary, a truly devoted person can come to one of the most expensive cities in the world, work long hours, and have no social life. It was a friend whom I'd met at Radcliffe who told me about the job I eventually landed as assistant to the managing editor at Pantheon/Schocken Books. Pantheon/Schocken is a prestigious publisher and imprint of Random House with a rich history that includes publishing such authors as Franz Kafka, John Berger, Simone de Beauvoir, Günter Grass, and Boris Pasternak. I was fortunate to work there while Andre Schiffrin was the editorial director, and under his stewardship I thought of Pantheon/ Schocken as a company with a mission. There seemed to be a strong belief that certain books should be published because they are worthwhile, great works and despite the fact that some of them may not be exceptionally profitable. It was a place of high standards with a commitment to literary works that was exhilarating to be around, and highly inspirational to a twenty-one-year-old novice in the industry. I had idealistic and romantic notions about what book publishers should publish, and it was great to be in an atmosphere that mirrored my commitment. And in a business very big on hierarchy and titles, I thought Andre seemed particularly interested in the younger staff. It was not business as usual.

Previous to working in publishing, owning hardcover books was a rare treat for me, and to suddenly be surrounded by and have access to these books was thrilling. On my very first day of the job, I remember standing before and admiring—almost salivating over—the many shelves of books, wondering if employees were allowed to take any of them free of charge. To my surprise Andre walked up behind me. I was afraid he had read my mind and knew I really wanted to read some of those books. He very kindly told me that I could have whichever books I wanted, reached down for a copy of *The Lover* by Marguerite Duras, handed it to me, and said, "You might like this. It is very good." I've been an avid Duras reader ever since.

The first year on the job, I was intimidated by the staff's literary acumen. Many of them held advanced degrees. Just out of school and having read nothing but the classics in high school and college, I became very aware of my limited knowledge of modern fiction. I was overwhelmed by the need to learn more about modern writers. It was during this time that I began to realize that although I was beginning my career in production, eventually I would become an acquisitions editor, because editorial work suited my interests more. As it turned out, beginning my publishing career in production made for a solid background in editorial.

Managing editors and their assistants link the editorial, design, and production departments. A good managing editor needs a certain type of personality in order to be effective. On a daily basis they must have extraordinary organizational skills, unimaginable tenacity, and a firm take-no-prisoners, in-your-face style that brings acquisitions editors to their knees. A managing editor's job differs from house to house, but generally it includes coordinating and supervising all the processes involved in making a book. This involves problem solving, troubleshooting, making sure everything gets done on time and within predetermined budgets, and checking all stages of copy from author, editor, and others. The assistant to the managing editor deals with almost all the different departments within a publishing house. The job gave me a good overall understanding of what is involved in making a book. I also learned to appreciate just how much the managing editor, production editors, and the production managers really do. This can be a somewhat mysterious process to acquisitions editors. I also did different kinds of computer work, attended and reported on the production meetings, kept all the scheduling information about every book on file in the computer, watched the backlist to see when books should be reprinted, and did any job that needed to be done to organize the book scheduling. It's an apprenticeship business and people learn by working closely with their bosses.

Still, it was all very foreign to me, and it took a long time to comprehend the whys and hows in the book production process from beginning to end. I also began to learn a new language: blads, blurbs, galleys, pages, blues, and so forth. And I quickly discovered, even though I didn't understand why, at first, that the relationship between managing editors and acquiring editors was inherently adversarial. Much of the managing editor's job consists of playing watchdog and making sure things flow as smoothly and efficiently as possible. Acquiring editors often don't have a true appreciation of how difficult a job this is and what is required of the managing editor. Instead, they often take this watchdog behavior as some kind of personal offense. As the managing editor's assistant, I was often caught in the middle of these forces when nudging and sometimes reprimanding editors about sloppy or late material. I loathed this part of the job. Editors would occasionally snap at me, close the door when they saw me coming, or pretend not to see me hovering in the doorway if they were on the phone. Managing editors have a tough time of it.

I started out making $14,000 a year and worked a lot of overtime. I liked and respected my boss; I loved being in an intellectual and literary atmosphere; and I felt happy and even privileged just to be around a lot of bright, highly educated, and accomplished people in the work environment. Many assistants worked second jobs to supplement their incomes, but I refused to do that. I had juggled three jobs in order to put myself through college; working the regular and overtime hours at Pantheon/Schocken, I just wasn't up for more. The majority of the assistants were women, and we became a tightly knit group. We had monthly "girls' night out" after-work drink dates to get to know one another.

The atmosphere at Pantheon/Schocken felt more like that of a small business than a large corporation. I remember one time after Andre returned from a trip to Asia, he'd had beautiful slides made from photos taken on the trip. He called a special lunch meeting where pizza was served, and we viewed the slides while he spoke about his travels.

The production/copy editors were an impressive bunch of the most accomplished, erudite people I had ever met. One man possessed a wit reminiscent of Oscar Wilde and occasionally held martini parties after work in his very small office. All of us would attend, invariably spilling out into the hallway.

Another unique aspect of working at Pantheon/Schocken was the variety of tasks assistants could participate in that did not fall under their particular job descriptions. For example, when I realized I was attracted to the editorial side, I was able to read manuscripts and give editorial reports about them to an editor who was generous and overworked. Assistants were encouraged to work on the Schocken paperback list, scouting small press and university press catalogs for books that might fit well into the line. If we saw something appropriate for the list, we were to contact the publisher, get the book, and decide whether to recommend it for the paperback list. This was a great opportunity for the young staff, and we were all excited about it.

Work was a safe haven for me that first turbulent year in New York City. It was a year of big adjustments, and working at Pantheon/Schocken Books was something that I could depend on. My boss, the managing editor, told me that there are three important things that dictate how you're faring in New York and whether a person new to the city decides to stay or leave—your working situation, your living situation, and your love life. If all three are lousy, you will pick up and go. After seven years in New York and witnessing the departure from the city of most of the people I knew in the Radcliffe publishing course, I have come to agree with her. You must feel good about at least one of these three things in order to stay. Some people bounced from publishing job to publishing job their first year in New York. I, on the other hand, was steadily employed, but plagued by the "crazy roommate syndrome." I moved six times that first year and hardly had any life outside of work, much less a love life. I was thankful for the stability my job gave me.

I am happy with my decision to work in book publishing despite the fact that the publishing industry still looks a lot like it did when I entered it seven years ago. There is regrettably very little racial and class diversity. I am often the only person of color in the editorial department, and this is quite unsettling in a city that has one million more people of color than it does white people. This industry needs people who reflect America's demographics. Publishing could be a far more attractive employment possibility to people of every socioeconomic group if the pay were better. I am part of the Open Book Committee at PEN American Center, which is devoted to raising public awareness of the lack of diversity in the book publishing industry. We have planned a publishing-day fair for junior and senior college students of color from the East to attend panel discussions about career paths in book publishing. The committee urges publishing insiders to acknowledge that there is a problem. Without first acknowledging this, there can be no change. Book publishing professionals have to realize that not only does the consumer miss out as a result of the lack of diversity, but the industry as a whole would prosper more with a serious commitment to being more inclusive. The consumer power of African-Americans and Latinos can no longer be ignored. I hope to achieve a position in a publishing company where I can influence recruiting practices and create a mentoring program. As one friend put it, "Publishing books without editors of color is like trying to play baseball without Jackie Robinson."

After seven years I am now an associate editor and am glad to have spent time in the production department my first year. I find the work rewarding, despite the frustrations of low pay and long hours and the type of stress created by a job where a lot depends on how well your most recent books have sold. It is very gratifying to be able to peer into the creative process, to learn a craft well, to work with ideas on a daily basis, and to work with writers in an artist-friendly environment.

I've seen friends leave book publishing only to come back to it. One of them, who left New York to work for the improvement of housing for poor people, called me up to say that he missed publishing and was surprised at how much we in the industry take for granted. He said, "You work on a very different level in the publishing business." Book publishing is exciting and interesting work, and feeling passionate about what you do is a privilege many people never experience.

Joy Smith was most recently an associate editor at Charles Scribner's Sons in New York. She was previously employed at Pantheon/Schocken Books and Crown Publishers, Inc. She has worked with authors such as the National Book Award winner E. Annie Proulx and American Book Award winner Bob Shacochis.

7

If You Won the Lottery

SYLVIA K. MILLER

While I was attending the New York University Summer Publishing Institute, my grandfather, who was helpless from two strokes, was in an expensive nursing home in California. My parents told me during one of my collect calls from a pay phone in the lobby of the dormitory that the money—his insurance, his and my parents' available savings—had run out. I was scared. How would I find a job and an apartment in New York with only the couple of hundred dollars I had left? My parents offered to scrape together enough to bring me home, but I did not want to go back to California yet. I wanted to work in book publishing in New York.

I had tried to find an entry-level publishing job when I graduated from the University of California, Berkeley, but even though there is a great deal of book publishing in California, most of the companies are quite small and do not have room for beginners. The only two that responded to my inquiry were North Point Press, which might have needed a freelance copy editor at some indefinite point in the future, and the University of California

Press, which had no openings at the time but would be glad to keep my résumé on file. I had majored in comparative literature and at the same time built an art portfolio in the hopes of becoming a graphic artist. I had spent a lot of time in Berkeley's wonderful career library to see if I could resolve these disparate interests in word and image into one vocation. I read pamphlets, listened to tapes, and took computer tests. One computer test advised me either to become a lawyer, because I liked words, or go into the military, because I liked structure. So much for *that* test. Another test digested my interests and "values" and decided that I should be an editor first, journalist second, and graphic artist last. I could tell that this was some pretty wise software.

A counselor told me about the three major summer publishing seminars in the United States in which professionals in the field teach you about different aspects of publishing in about six weeks and help you find a publishing job. To cover all the bases, I applied to all three—Denver, Radcliffe, and NYU—but I was most excited about NYU. Looking at an aerial photograph in the NYU brochure showing the Washington Square arch and Fifth Avenue stretching north from it, I exclaimed to my roommate, "Barbara, look, that's the center of the world!" Barbara smiled at me as if I were really off my rocker, but my parents had brought me up on the *New Yorker* and exciting trips to take in New York City's museums and concerts, and even though I might have sounded like an innocent, I meant what I said. The funny thing is that after eight years in Manhattan the excitement is still there. (The center may have shifted slightly northwest, settling on Broadway somewhere between Lincoln Center and Shakespeare & Co. Booksellers, but let's not quibble.) NYU sent me a fat envelope with an acceptance letter and information about dormitories, and I found that I had made my big decision. New York, here we come!

Having graduated from Cal Berkeley in December, I had six

months to save up some money before the NYU program started in late June, so I took the first job I could find, as a receptionist/ advertising assistant in a San Francisco financial company. My job included not only handling a busy switchboard and helping write and design advertising but also making the coffee, serving it in each person's favorite mug, and washing the dirty mugs. I was a good sport, because I had a secret: I was not interested in big-equipment financing; in six months I was going to New York to become an editor.

One evening per week, I took a continuing-education course in Berkeley that perked me up. It was an introduction to publishing taught by Malcolm Margolin, a Berkeley publisher with a long, flowing beard. The NYU seminar later taught me a lot about big-time publishing, but no course I ever took taught me as much as this one about the true value of book publishing and the process of book production. Mr. Margolin taught us why a manuscript should be copyedited, how to make a light table for laying out pages, how to turn galleys into pages with scissors and rubber cement; he showed us his typesetting machines in action, explained how to distribute a small-press book yourself, and treated our own book ideas with respectful practicality. He taught us how to iden-tify a "right book," one in which idea, purpose, size, type, and design all fit perfectly together to make an object that has a kind of magic about it. Book publishing was ideas, words, art, construc-tion—everything I liked best. I would enter the class tired, feeling the weight of a long day's work and a commute by bus, and I would leave with my feet not quite touching the ground. Mr. Margolin's favorite typeface, Garamond, is still my favorite, too.

I am a careful person, and I like to confirm my instincts through research. The continuing-education course in Berkeley confirmed that I wanted to go to the NYU Summer Publishing Institute, which in turn confirmed that I wanted to work in book, not magazine, publishing and furthermore that I wanted to work on scholarly books, not the trade books and best-sellers that all the other students were so excited about. Finding a job, it turned out, was not difficult. I pursued some listings in the NYU publishing job file and was offered a position as an editorial assistant at a trade paperback publisher. As I interviewed and took a line-editing test for this job, I tried to convince myself that working on cookbooks, romances, and westerns would be fun, but when the job was actually offered to me, I just couldn't accept it. I was afraid that another would not come along before my money ran out, but one did.

During my interview for an assistant position with Lloyd Chilton, executive editor in the Professional and Reference Books Division at Macmillan, he asked me if I wouldn't rather be in trade publishing. I was very certain of my answer and even told him about the job I had not taken. In my interview with the managing editor, Elyse Dubin, who would share an assistant with Mr. Chilton, I talked a mile a minute and showed her the eight-page brochure I had produced, when I wasn't washing coffee mugs, for the leasing company in San Francisco. I don't know if hardly letting your prospective supervisor get a word in edgewise is the best interviewing technique, but I was enthusiastic about the prospect of working with scholarly books on higher education, music, history, and religion. As I walked out of the building I realized that this was the job that I really wanted. Fortunately, I wasn't on tenterhooks for very long; later the same day the woman in the Macmillan personnel department told me that Mr. Chilton and Ms. Dubin wanted to offer me the job because I had "knocked their socks off." I was *in!*

The NYU summer institute ended on a Friday, and my new job began the following Monday, a smooth transition. Finding a place to live was another story. When a fellow student returned home to Texas on Friday, she bequeathed me a jar of peanut butter. Trying to conserve my money so that I could rent an apartment, I lived for several days on this peanut butter along with crackers taken from the student cafeteria and hoarded. Peanut butter for breakfast, peanut butter for lunch, peanut butter for dinner; but it was no use, because I did not have enough money for a rent deposit on even the most depressing apartments that I saw—a small studio to share with a woman who was out of work, a room in an almost renovated loft with an electric hot plate to share, an apartment to share in a dangerous-looking Brooklyn neighborhood reached by a long ride in a fiery-hot, graffiti-covered train. Just before my time in the dormitory ran out, I found the Markle Residence on a tree-lined Greenwich Village street, an affordable residence for women run by the Salvation Army that had a cafeteria, weekly maid service, and a roof garden. Even with my starting salary of $13,500 per year, I could afford to share a room there. The "intake supervisor" soon found an opening for me, if only to make me stop calling her.

Entry-level jobs are available, and you will find one. Unfortunately, it will pay you very little. I disapprove greatly of the I-had-to-walk-five-miles-to-school-every-day-in-the-snow-with-no-boots-so-you-shouldn't-complain attitude prevalent in publishing. Entry-level salaries are creeping upward, but they are still, for the most part, almost unlivable. I compared carefully the prices of sandwich bags (for my peanut-butter-cracker lunches), and I spent fifty cents on coffee only on Fridays. Be prepared: Get an evening job, ask your parents to help you as if this were graduate school, share an apartment, and if you are a woman, call the John and Mary Markle Evangeline Residence. I lived there three years.

It was the perfect first job for someone who was interested in everything and wasn't sure if she wanted to be an acquisitions editor, like Lloyd Chilton, or a managing editor, like Elyse Dubin.

An acquisitions editor goes out and finds authors, persuades the publisher to gamble on them, and works with them to develop a finished manuscript. A managing editor sees the manuscript through the design, copyediting, and proofreading stages and turns it into a book. For Lloyd, I typed contract requests and his admirably to-the-point letters, and I helped him keep track of everything. This is what an assistant to an acquisitions editor does. For Elyse, I checked corrections on proofs, sent packages of manuscripts and galleys to freelance copy editors and to authors, and learned to mark manuscripts and proofs clearly for the typesetter. This is what an assistant to a managing editor does. Lloyd told me that a contract request always comes first, because contracts should be offered to authors as soon as possible before they have a chance to change their minds. Elyse told me that production deadlines always come first because the bound-book date must not slip. I did everything as fast as I could.

I asked a thousand questions, and no one seemed to mind. I asked Lloyd how he estimated expenses and income for his proposed projects, and I asked Elyse why there is a slash next to a proofreading symbol, when to use close-up marks, and how to read type specifications. Lloyd let me try my hand at editing the introduction to a book and writing catalog copy, and Elyse lent me three grammar books to study because somehow in all my grand education no one had ever taught me that there are specific rules for where commas belong and where they don't.

Somewhere along the way I was promoted to senior editorial assistant, and Elyse assigned me my first book to supervise through the production process. That meant I hired a copy editor and supervised her work; sent the edited manuscript to the author; and incorporated the author's final changes and responses to queries correctly and neatly, in a way that a typesetter could understand. Meanwhile, I filled out a design-survey form for the production department identifying all the elements in the book that needed to be designed and assigning each a code—"CT" for chapter titles and "I" for first-order heading, and so on. I read the type specifications prepared by the designer to make sure they would work and, along with the acquisitions editor, approved the typeset design samples. When the copyedited manuscript was ready for typesetting, each element was coded so that the typesetter would know which type specification to use for each. The copy editor could code the manuscript, but it was my responsibility to make sure it was done correctly.

About a month to six weeks later, the production department—sometimes called the manufacturing department, to distinguish its job from the one I was doing in "editorial production"—gave me typeset galley proofs from the compositor, the outside company chosen to typeset and eventually make pages for this particular book. I sent the galleys to the author for proofreading along with strict instructions to mark only "printer's"— that is, typesetter's—errors, called "pe's," and not to make other changes, called "aa's," for "author's alterations." Inevitably, the author made other alterations anyway but probably not enough to exceed his allowance per contract, 10 percent of the cost of composition, a sum almost impossible to calculate in advance, especially because one could not be sure how much the alterations themselves would cost. Only a practiced eye could tell if the galleys had too many marks on them.

Page proofs appeared about a month after the galleys, to be checked against the galleys to ensure the corrections had been made properly. Checking corrections was the first task Elyse gave me on my first day at Macmillan, although with smaller books this task was usually given to the author, who would prepare an index at the same time. After a cover design from the production department had been approved by me, Elyse, and the acquisitions editor, and after the camera-ready pages had been checked one last time, the production department packed everything off to the printer. In about two weeks, the bluelines arrived, copies of the negatives prepared by the printer on the kind of paper architects use for blueprint plans. Only crucial editorial errors could be fixed at this stage; the "blues," as they are called for short, are for checking that all the parts of the book are in order and that there are not any imperfections like spots or broken type on the negatives from which the plates will be made. The blues gave off a slight chemical smell that eventually made me a bit dizzy because I had my nose so close to them. I wasn't going to miss any spots. Later I learned that it is better not to drive the printer crazy by marking tiny imperfections on every other page; you might distract the printer's staff from making the most important corrections properly. About six weeks later I held in my hand the book that I had made.

I liked this project, and when an opening came along, I was promoted first to production associate and then to editorial supervisor. My job consisted of supervising the process I just described for about twelve books at a time on a variety of subjects: higher education administration, history, religion, and music. The books were called "professional" books because they were intended for an audience of scholars, or professionals, in their respective fields. Many of them were books that I had helped Lloyd initiate, giving me the opportunity to work on some books from the beginning to the end of the publishing process. The books were interesting, scholarly, and educational, definitely worth the material they were made of. I would never want to work on books that were not worth cutting down trees for. But eventually I began to feel bored. To use my mind in more creative ways, I began attending Columbia University in the evenings, working toward a master's degree in comparative literature. I considered becoming a professor only briefly, however; I planned to figure out some way to use my more advanced knowledge of the literature field in my publishing career. I still enjoyed editorial production, but something was missing, and I wondered if I would not prefer a job more like Lloyd's after all.

Claude Conyers, who had left our department to head the reference department at Oxford University Press, told me at lunch one day how an encyclopedia is developed. Our department produced thematic encyclopedias—notably the *Encyclopedia of Religion*, which had been supervised by Claude—but I had been involved with them only once, when Charles Smith, the publisher, gave me a research assignment to help an editorial board of Israeli scholars develop the table of contents for the *Encyclopedia of the Holocaust*. This was an exciting assignment, and it piqued my interest in encyclopedias. Claude described how an idea becomes a grid showing all aspects of the subject in time and space, so that the table of contents and article lengths can be perfectly balanced at the planning stage. He said he could see that my eyes were shining at the idea of doing this kind of creative work, but I must first learn how an encyclopedia is produced by being a project editor, he advised me.

Because I believe in doing things one step at a time, I applied for an opening in multivolume reference at Macmillan as soon as I could. As a project editor, I learned how to handle a manuscript twenty times longer than any I had dealt with before, with great numbers of authors and freelancers, a huge pile of illustrations, a whole wall of galleys belonging to a single project, in this case *The Coptic Encyclopedia*, a work so erudite and specialized that I think everyone was surprised when we actually sold a respectable number of the eight-volume sets.

Before this encyclopedia was published, though, I had moved again, this time to become a managing editor in the Scribner imprint, a similar job but with more independence, books in my own field of literature, and the opportunity to pursue my own ideas. As I did when I worked for Lloyd and Elyse, I still have a hybrid job, supervising editorial production and acquiring new books at the same time. I have not found job categories to be terribly rigid in publishing, especially in the small departments in which I have worked. When you want to do something new, the opportunity will be there, although sometimes you have to reach out and do extra work for a while to show that you can do it, and your new skills will be recognized and your responsibilities enlarged more officially later on.

Previously, I worked briefly on many books at once, never getting to know any one subject well. Now I work on only a few encyclopedias at one time, each for a year and a half to three years. I learn the subject, and sometimes it's a surprising one I wouldn't have pursued otherwise, like arms control and disarmament. I get to know the scholar who serves as general editor and adviser quite well. Production schedules can be demanding, with deadlines that seem impossible to meet, and we must often work terribly fast. Nevertheless, there is the feeling of an expanse of time during which the project becomes a significant part of your life. And the purpose of the books, whose main market is school, college, and public libraries, is not only to edify scholars but to help high school and college students learn something and write good term papers. Our highest goal is to publish a work that is substantial enough to be useful to scholars and clear and appealing enough to help students learn.

An encyclopedia on a certain subject defines a field of study and summarizes all the scholarship that has ever been contributed to it. To organize and wrap up an entire field is very satisfying. Of course each subject is a living thing, straining to burst out of our neatly tied ribbons—you can imagine, for example, what it was like to produce an *Encyclopedia of Arms Control and Disarmament* while the Soviet Union was breaking up—but if we do a good job, the set will stay in libraries for ten years or longer. The early volumes of the *Dictionary of American Biography* have been in libraries since 1929.

If I weren't an editor, I would be a teacher. In fact, an editor *is* a teacher. Every day I teach scholar-authors, ever so gently, how to clarify their material for our audience. I teach in-house staff and freelance copy editors intricate style points peculiar to each project and how to word author queries with a combination of authority and utmost deference. I am constantly training new free-lancers and at the same time learning from the experienced ones who have been editing since I was in grade school. When I have an idea for a new encyclopedia, I become a student of that subject until I can invent a tentative table of contents and talk intelligently about it with scholars who might serve on the proposed project's editorial board. There is always more to learn—about the subject of the encyclopedia and about editing.

What does my assistant do? He reviews and corrects copyedit-ing, he incorporates authors' responses to copyediting into final manuscripts for typesetting, he checks corrections on proofs, he speaks very politely to authors on the telephone, he does a lot of photocopying and mailing of packages, he types correspondence, and he keeps track of everything. He is learning quickly and will be able to run an encyclopedia project on his own one day soon. What are the qualifications for such a job? Education, intelligence, and a commitment to—or at least a strong interest in—publishing as a career. Neat, small handwriting and very good manners are definite pluses.

When you are looking for an entry-level publishing job, look for books that interest you, but even more important, look for a boss who will be a teacher. Although I turned up my nose at trade paperbacks, that job could have taught me skills transferable to scholarly publishing. Entry-level skills are transferable; it's only later that you will specialize. You might look for a large company or a small one, a trade publisher or a scholarly one, but remember: What that company will be to you is the people with whom you will work day in and day out. One of those people, preferably your immediate supervisor, should be your mentor. Publishing is still an apprenticeship business; you will learn it from the bottom up, and you will be glad that you had the patience to do so because your knowledge of all the details will give you confidence.

Of course every job has its drawbacks, and each day brings its pesky problems, but when all is said and done there are very few careers in the world that are as satisfying as publishing. Don't tell my boss, but I think that doing worthwhile and enjoyable work and actually getting paid for it is a tremendous privilege. If you are going to spend eight or more hours per day doing something to make a living, you might as well love it. The true test is, if you won the lottery, what would you do? I would edit reference books.

Sylvia K. Miller is senior editor with Charles Scribner's Sons Reference Books and Twayne Publishers, both imprints of Paramount Publishing. For Scribners, she edits thematic encyclopedias and is currently working on two supplements to the Dictionary of American Biography, British Writers Supplement III, American Nature Writers *(two volumes), and* Civilizations of the Ancient Near East *(four volumes). For Twayne, she edits three series of books in literary criticism.*

8

First Steps

VICTORIA KLOSE

You'd think writing about your first job in book publishing would be a snap. On reflection, however, it caused me a fair amount of writer's block because it meant reviewing my life, going back to a time when both this writer and many in publishing were more naive and less commercially aware.

I was a recent graduate of the University of Michigan, having earned a degree in English literature. Since a B.A. in English lit was not at all marketable in those days, the joke was: Those who can't, teach English. So I spent an incredibly rewarding three years teaching English in Barcelona to Catalanes, who desperately needed the language for higher education and for commerce. As is so often the case, the teacher learned much more than her students. I never suspected that all the grammar and endless parsing and diagramming of sentences the nuns taught me at private school would serve not only in my first freelance job but would also turn out to be the basis of my career as a copy editor and manager in publishing.

In the intervening twenty years, the mandate for copy editors has changed. Once, copy editors checked for spelling, grammar, punctuation, styled for consistency, and did light fact checking. Now, copy editors do all that as well as everything from minor revisions to major rewrites.

From my point of view, copyediting can be broken down into four discrete parts that sum up book publishing (the four food groups, if you will, of this industry): people, cooperation, communication, and vision/judgment.

The people a freelancer knows are the most important thing in her life. In the copyediting and proofreading classes I teach, I urge my students to get to know those sitting on either side of them. You never know where your next job will come from, and you certainly never know which colleague will jump from one house to another, leaving a slot to be filled or needing an assistant to go with her to the new position. In order to get ahead in publishing, you often have to change houses several times. I fit one of publishing's stereotypes: the house hopper.

I had a series of wonderful interviews with William Morrow and was certain a job offer was imminent, but I didn't hear another word for six months. Finally, the chief copy editor called to ask if I could help out on a freelance basis, and I, of course, jumped at this chance. I started out helping a best-selling author alphabetize an index he had prepared.

This author tried to involve his daughter in the project by explaining to her at length the distinction in indexes between "see" and "see also." Little did he know he was providing his Morrow assistant (me) with invaluable information she had never heard of till then, but which has served her in good stead ever since. It took another three months of freelancing for Morrow before a staff position opened up and I was hired—as the lowest person on the copyediting totem pole: the proofreader.

It was as proofreader that I honed my tools of the trade—basic copyediting symbols—and learned to speak the vocabulary of copyediting. When a senior editor with twenty years' experience asked me when those "long skinny funny things" were coming in, I knew she was asking about galleys. I learned what "slugging" meant (comparing galleys to page proofs and page proofs to repros). I learned to collate galleys (incorporate author's corrections into a master set). I learned that only major bloopers (e.g., misspelling an author's name or book title) should be corrected in blues.

Morrow had a bull pen setup for its copy editors, so I realized in that first year that while copy editors have a reputation of being straitlaced and easily shocked, as a group they in fact have a wonderful sense of humor. (Betsy Cenedella, one of the best copy editors around, regaled me with my first "copyediting" joke: Two little old white-haired women copy editors had offices across from each other. One day, Mary looked up and asked, "Mildred, is 'motherfucker' one word or two?") Most copy editors also have areas of expertise that range from "normal" (going on archaeological digs) to exotic (belly dancing at parties). They all have a love of words and can spend hours discussing the etymology of a given word and whether it should be capped or lowercased, italicized or left roman.

You move from proofreader to department head usually by being very good at what you do, but mainly by being very lucky. Staff copy editors rarely move on, so the attrition rate is almost nonexistent. I became Morrow's chief copy editor because several people retired and because more senior department members didn't want the job. I had also, unbeknownst to me, passed what I call a baptism of paper.

While my boss was on vacation, I ran the department. Morrow had contracted to do an anthology of some early short stories by

Erle Stanley Gardner. Because of Morrow's long-standing relationship with Gardner (Morrow had published him from the beginning), his widow was given a set of galleys for review and approval. She returned them so heavily corrected it was almost impossible to decipher her changes. Without getting upset and after a few phone conversations with her, decipher and incorporate them I did. Gardner's editor, Narcisse Chamberlain, was impressed by my grace under fire and put in a good word for me with the higher-ups. For the next five years, I managed Morrow's in-house copyediting staff of six and a freelance staff of copy editors, proofers, and indexers of about thirty people.

It turned out that in those years my reputation had somehow preceded me (something I never thought about in the tumult of getting the best copyediting, proofing, and indexing possible for the more than two hundred titles a year that came through my office), and I was subsequently wooed away from William Morrow by Random House. (As it so happened, the man who hired me had worked closely with one of my brothers on the *Washington Post*.) While my responsibilities as chief copy editor at Random House were similar to what I had done at Morrow, I also had been hired because of my attitude and management style.

At that time, Random House's copyediting department was mired in negativism. I'm a great believer in politeness and in cooperating with those around me, so I successfully changed that department's "never will" attitude to an "I'll give it a try" can-do attitude. I was very successful at this.

The highly regarded publisher who had recommended me to Random House had herself jumped houses and mentioned me to Bantam Books, which was in need of a manager with my expertise. Bantam then offered me an expanded position of supervising a vast managing editor's department, overseeing a cover-copy department in desperate need of restructuring, and acting as an in-house operational-systems troubleshooter and streamliner.

I was hired away from Bantam by Morrow—where I had started out ten years before—to do for Morrow what I had been doing for Bantam. It used to be that three jumps were enough; that the third was the last. That's not true anymore. Book publishing is not recessionproof, and I, unfortunately, also fit the description of another industry stereotype—the one who has been downsized out of a career. In twenty years I have come full circle and am back in the bosom of the freelance community, vying with all the other talent that's out there. With all the layoffs and downsizings, there's a lot of stiff competition.

Freelancers deal with people every day, but for a freelance copy editor, it's the chief copy editors, managing editors, and production editors who give her work. One of my former colleagues from Barcelona gave me my very first freelance job when I returned to the United States to start my "real" life. I knew I had a facility for language and that I was a stickler for detail, but I didn't know if that would translate into anything resembling a career. Fortunately, it did.

Mary Vaughn, then managing editor of Regents Publishing, needed someone to copyedit a line of ESL (English as a Second Language) books. I had contacted Mary when I got back to the States, and she thought of me for this project. I took Mary's copy-editing test—not knowing a Harvard comma from a serial comma from no serial comma at all—and was put to work. My relationship with Mary through the years has reinforced my faith in the power of cultivating contacts. You never know when one professional relationship will lead to another. I worked for Mary on a slew of books and parlayed that experience into other contacts at other houses.

Our reputations are only as good as our own performance and

those of the people we hire, whether they are full time or freelance. Mary gave me the chance that all of us starting out need. From listening to her and from reading style books (*Words into Type, The Chicago Manual of Style*) on the side, I learned what a serial comma was; what "flopped" meant when applied to artwork; what to do with bottom-of-the-page footnotes; how to check page proofs, repros, and blues. The main thing I learned that first year was the importance of staying in touch with my employer and not being bashful about asking her for more work or asking her for the names of others whom I could contact. Most of the recommendations freelancers get are from those for whom they've worked, so a freelance editor must overcome shyness to network because that's the only way to build a broad client base.

I also learned the inestimable value of communicating. A chief copy editor has a responsibility to provide professional critiques—good and bad—of her freelancers' work. Otherwise, you might find yourself being irritated by having to repeatedly correct something a freelancer might not know about styling. While I thought of them as personalized tutorials in copyediting, a lot of my freelancers called my missives schoolmarm letters.

By the same token, the freelancer has an obligation to inform her employer if there is a problem with the manuscript or if she can't meet a deadline. (I once assigned a manuscript about child abuse to a copy editor who had two young daughters. We talked at length about the subject matter and its possible impact, but she assured me it wouldn't be a problem to copyedit this. She was wrong. A week later, she called to say she couldn't believe what she was reading and couldn't handle copyediting this project. Every time she looked at her innocent young daughters, she burst into tears. Her decision to give back the manuscript was the best thing for her, and it still gave me enough time to reassign it.) The last thing a chief copy editor wants is to be facing a critical deadline and discover the job hasn't been done. That leaves the chief copy editor without any options for achieving drop-dead schedules.

A good copy editor sees the whole work and exercises judgment with every manuscript, and this judgment comes with the realization that book publishing is a cooperative effort. (It's been my experience that most copy editors are women, so I use "she" and "her" advisedly.) She is there to make the manuscript as good as it possibly can be. She's not there to rework a manuscript in her own image and likeness but to make what's there sing. She should know how much *to* do as well as how much *not* to do. She should be able to recognize serviceable, nonaward-winning prose (most of what is published) from delightfully written fiction or nonfiction. Sometimes this balance is precarious, and sometimes it comes naturally with the material. For example, a copy editor with judgment is not going to agonize over the stylistic points in a bodice buster (romance) or boy book (action adventure). She is simply going to style everything consistently and enjoy and appreciate the material for what it is. She should not impose her personal taste for literary writing on this kind of manuscript. With literary writing, however, a copy editor with judgment *will* agonize over whether the word "eager" (positively enthusiastic) was meant instead of "anxious" (awaiting with trepidation and fear). Instinctively knowing just what should be done in a manuscript is what separates really good copy editors from average ones, and these above-average kinds are few and far between.

Judgment extends to the sorts of queries a copy editor might have for an author, and this relates to communication. More often than not, a copy editor will never meet the author whose manuscript she is editing. When phrasing a marginal query for an author, the copy editor should, therefore, remember the four-letter word of publishing: "tact." Sometimes it's not *what* you say but *how* you say it. An author will respond more positively to a copy editor's query or change if given the reason behind it, and copy editors should always have a good reason for changing anything in a manuscript. They must never forget they are there to enhance the manuscript and as merely one part of a multifaceted cooperative process.

People communicating with each other leads to cooperation. Cooperation, in turn, leads to vision/judgment. A copy editor's primary function is to pay attention to the minutiae of a work without losing sight of the larger, more global theme or subject matter. A copy editor should understand and appreciate how an author's diction (in the old-fashioned sense of the word; that is, choice of words) and use of punctuation—a comma here, a semicolon there—are crucial; how each and every "minor" detail of an author's creation progresses word by word, perhaps logically and sometimes beautifully, from one phrase to another; that those phrases make up a lovely sentence and that these sentences evolve into a startling paragraph; that paragraph after paragraph build one on top of the other to create the characters, mood, voice, tone, and reality of a unified whole. Imagine the wordsmithship of Wallace Stegner or Maya Angelou, of Davis Grubb or Toni Morrison; think of the care with which such writers pick over the rubble of language to make a self-sustaining structure. Think of those who evoke every emotion felt by man and who do so with utmost grace and wit. A good copy editor will savor these details and understand how they build to a crescendo of motive, characterization, dramatic tension, and denouement. The same good copy editor will see the forest *and* the trees.

People, cooperation, communication, and vision/judgment— all these things I gleaned from my very first copyediting job. The lessons learned have served me in good stead, and they are lessons I try to impart to others.

Most of us are in publishing because we cherish language, because we're fascinated by the creativity or perseverance of others; because we're allowed to be eccentric and offbeat and can try something new; because publishing is a world of ideas—good ones and bad ones; ones we agree with and ones we oppose; ones that are beautifully expressed and others that are not—and ideas, after all, are the most seductive things on Earth.

Victoria Klose, a cofounder of K&N Bookworks, a book producer, is also a freelance copy editor and publishing/management consultant. She teaches at New York University's Center for Publishing.

9

Beautiful Enough to Be Unnoticed

CLAIRE NAYLON VACCARO

The salary was wretched, but I was thrilled to have found a job as a designer in the publishing industry. My father thought I was nuts for taking this job instead of the one for the Metropolitan Transit Authority organizing slide presentations and designing signage, which paid much more money. All he knew was that I was going to owe a lot of money in student loans once I finished my master's degree. All I knew was that I loved books and hardly knew anything about what went into making them.

I was in my last year of graduate school at Pratt Institute when I ran out of money to pay for school. I had only my thesis to complete, but that would take a year and a good deal of money. During the three years I had been at Pratt in the Communication Design Master's Program, I often heard this little voice in my head saying, "How am I ever going to make a living at this when I get out of here?" That last year there were two reasons I knew I had to start looking for my first real design job. The first was so that I could afford to finish my thesis and the second was to find out if I really could make a living at design before leaving the security of school life, which I had already prolonged by going to graduate school instead of diving into "the real world" right after college. (Oh, my god—what if I had done that?)

I sent résumés for every design assistant job I could find listed in the *New York Times*. I went on many interviews, some at small design studios, some at advertising agencies, and some at publishing houses. The first publishing company at which I interviewed told me I couldn't be an assistant if I had no experience (hah!). The second publishing interview was for an assistant's job in children's books at Random House. As I headed into the human resources department, I had a really good feeling. I had been to so many interviews that I was starting to feel a sort of reckless confidence. I had also just had my second good interview with the MTA, so I was starting to feel as if I might be able to end my search soon. (Fate is amazing. I realize now that walking into this Random House interview shaped the rest of my life.)

"That job has already been filled," the personnel woman told me. Her name was Sherri; I had sent her a cover letter and résumé for the assistant's job. She had called me in, so I guess she felt bad that she had nothing open. She invited me into her office and asked if she could see my portfolio anyway, maybe offer me some interviewing tips. Since there was no longer a job to be filled, I relaxed and had a good time showing off all the school projects that made up my portfolio. After viewing my portfolio, Sherri got on the phone to Virginia Tan, the design director of Alfred A. Knopf, an imprint of Random House. Ms. Tan had also been looking for a new assistant but thought she had found one. Sherri told her she had someone who was very interested in working in publishing and pretty much said, "Please see her."

So up I went to the twentieth floor to be interviewed for a job I knew nothing about. What I remember most about that interview was the incredible view from Ms. Tan's corner-office windows. She was kind enough to wade patiently through my school projects and listen to my detailed explanations about each one.

I left her office thinking happily, "Well, if that doesn't work out, at least I'm still in the running for the MTA job and at least I met some really nice people."

I got two phone calls the next day. One was from the MTA guy saying I had made the cut from one hundred people down to ten. He was planning on interviewing again and cutting down to four before he made his decision. I was a little excited but also wondered, "What if I really get this job? Do I really want this job?" Until then I had just wanted a *job* but had never really thought I might have a choice. The second call was from Virginia Tan asking me if I would like to work for her at Knopf. I was really excited. I told her I would think about it and let her know my answer in a couple of days. I pictured myself at each job in five years, and that is how I made my decision about which one to take. The next day I accepted the job as design assistant at Knopf. Although I wasn't aware of it at the time, this was a very special place to begin a career in book design.

I felt like such a kid my first day on the job. Virginia took me to a room across the hall from hers and said, "Here is your office." I was shocked. "My own office; I get my very own office?" She laughed at me and said it would soon be filled with work.

After that she took me down the hall to a stat camera room. She showed me how to work the camera and then set me up making photostats of slides for a book she was working on that day. I spent the entire day in that little dark room smelling stat chemicals and starving. Virginia came back near the end of the day and said, "I hope you don't think that this is all you'll be doing. It's just that I really needed those stats today. Tomorrow you'll find out a lot more about what you'll be doing. One of the designers, Marysarah, will show you around tomorrow."

Marysarah turned out to be my best friend. She made it all seem fun and relaxed. After the second day I felt at home in my new job. Marysarah had held my position previously, so she knew what I was responsible for. The first thing we did was order supplies. She let me order everything I wanted plus everything she knew I would need. I remember telling her I needed a protractor (I'd never had one, and it looked cool). She didn't blink an eye, and we ordered one. That protractor still sits in my desk drawer and has never been used. One of my tasks would be to keep the department stocked with all the supplies the staff needed.

There were six designers on staff, and I would be assisting all of them with whatever they needed so I could learn my way around book design. Marysarah, who knew from experience that you just have to jump right in, handed me my first photo insert to lay out. It took me about two days of staring at the photos before I figured out what a photo insert really is and started working on it.

Another designer, Iris, had me patching in tiny pieces of type to the repro of a book she was working on. The repro, or reproduction proof, is the mechanical stage of the book that goes to the printer, so everything must be perfect at this point. If there is any scratched or crooked type on the repro, it will show up in the final book. I remember bringing her one page of the book *at least* six times, and each time she would say, "It's still not perfect." She had me photocopy it so I could see it better, and of course she was right; the type was a tiny bit too much to the left, or right, or crooked, or the letters were spaced unevenly. I really learned a lot from her about perfection. At the time I complained bitterly (to myself, of course), but there have been a couple of times in the past seven years when I have done the same thing to someone who was working for me. Iris taught me to have a hawk's eye for crooked or off-center type.

I remember when the book—*The Debutante* by Gioia Diliberto —was published. I saw it in a bookstore window on the Upper West Side. I was exclaiming to my friend, "Look, I worked on that book!" when a woman standing next to me with her husband and baby said, "Really? I wrote that book! I'm Gioia!" It was very funny, especially since I then had to explain the very small role I had played in its publication, but it was still very exciting.

Each of the six designers at Knopf was amazing in her or his own way, so in the beginning I sat and watched them a lot and looked through many of the books they had designed. I sat with Dorothy while she picked binding colors for one of her books; it was a big decision. Once, while she was away, I had to get the repro for one of her cookbooks ready to go to the printer, and there was an ornament missing from the book. It was my most important decision yet. I had to pick an ornament for her design and hope that it would be what she wanted! (She liked my selection.)

Over the next few months I began to learn that book design is a subtle art form that a lot of people don't know much about. I had always loved books and collected them. Some I just collected as objects, never intending to read them. I made books when I was a child, and I made books for a few of my projects in college and graduate school. Everything about this new job held great interest for me. I'm still not bored with it seven years later.

After a few weeks, Virginia gave me my first book to design all by myself. Marysarah walked me through every step. There was so much to learn. Sure I had gone to college for design and graduate school for design, but nobody taught me all there is to making a book. I remember asking Marysarah, "Can I make the title like this?" or "Can I make the folios do that?" and she replied over and over, "Sure you can. You're the designer." I had never felt that freedom in school, and it's that freedom that makes it so much fun to design.

Of course, somewhere along the way I learned that you hit snags in that beautiful freedom. I remember for my first book design I searched for days for a typeface to use for the title page and chapter titles. I found exactly what I wanted, made my layouts, and showed them to Virginia; she liked them; and then it was time for me to have my first meeting with an editor. The editor liked them, and I was on my way. Snnnaaaggggg! That beautiful typeface I had chosen was nowhere to be found—it wasn't made anymore—and there was no way I could use it. It was a brutal lesson, but I got over it. I spent a long time searching for the next most "perfect" typeface and eventually found the one I liked.

The next thing I had to do was *spec the manuscript*. This task sent me into fits of terror. In school, both undergraduate and graduate, my professors made a big scary deal about this ominous type-speccing skill students were required to master. If you didn't do it really well, you were bound to go nowhere in life. Yet they barely touched on it anywhere in the curriculum. I think they spent perhaps one day showing us how to fit one block of copy onto a fake ad, and then they included the same exercise on a final exam! That was my type-speccing education. But I nervously answered, "Yes," when asked in my job interviews if I could spec type. I remember telling Virginia, "Well, yeah, I've specced a little type here and there." (It was true. I had.)

Type speccing is really quite simple. It means describing to the typesetter in your very own language exactly what you want done with the type in your design. Be extremely specific in your instructions (your specs), and that's pretty much all there is to it. Speccing an entire manuscript is a little different from speccing a little block of copy, but now that I do it all the time, I can laugh. With a lot of help, I specced my first manuscript, and it was sent off to the typesetter.

Another of my duties as the assistant was to process the paperwork for the department and make sure freelancers got paid. The designers sometimes hired freelancers to make a map, or make mechanicals, or provide some illustrations. It took me quite a while to get into the habit of handling this duty, mostly because I was so involved with doing what I liked, designing. Now that I am a freelancer, I am grateful to the people who pay me in a reasonable amount of time. Now I wish I had been more diligent in this part of my job.

With each new book I designed, I was faced with a new set of problems to solve. In the beginning, every little part of every design was precious to me. For a book called *Therapeutic Touch,* I made an ornament to decorate the end of every chapter. I felt that it was a really good ornament for the book, but there was no way of knowing if the editor would feel the same way. I was relieved that she liked the design and didn't even mention the ornament. That's the way it should be. The design should be beautiful enough to be unnoticed, not worth mentioning. I guess that sounds a little funny. You would think most designers design something to be noticed, but that's not true in book design. The most important thing to do when designing a book is to make it as comfortable for the reader as possible. As I showed my layouts to the editors, I learned how to explain to them why I did what I did and how the book made me feel. I also learned what some editors liked and disliked, and that helped in designing their books in the future. I learned how a very simple design could be very difficult to create, but that ultimately that simplicity would be best for the book.

One of the first books I designed was called *Letters to Olga* by Vaclav Havel. It was a collection of letters the author had written to his wife while he was in prison. The book was divided into four parts. The parts marked the passage of time, which I wanted to show on the part-title pages. I made the part titles white type in a black box. On the first part the box hung from the top of the page, on the second it hung lower, on the third it floated low on the page, and on the fourth it hit the bottom of the page. This approach was subtle, but it accomplished what I wanted without being too prominent.

Now, when I look back at the books I designed in the beginning of my career, I'm very proud of them. As I learned more and designed more books, I got much more adventurous and started to have a lot of fun. It's always a challenge to see how I can make a book look special without going overboard. Most people, when they're reading a book, don't realize that someone sat down and thought hard about what the page numbers should look like or what typeface should be used for the text. Sometimes I look back and think, "I can't believe I did that. I really overdid it." And sometimes I think, "That's pretty cool. Did I do that?"

When my first book design was printed and bound as a real book, I was thrilled. Until then, my family had not really understood what I was doing at my job, so this made it much easier to explain; plus the book had my name in the back, and for some reason that made them excited too. That first book design is still part of my portfolio.

Whenever I tell anyone I'm a book designer, the usual response is, "Oh, you do the covers." And then I go into my explanation that although I do design covers occasionally, as well as other graphic design pieces, book design is my main job and what I really love to do. It's been seven years, so I've gotten used to explaining my profession. Most people seem really interested when I describe all the things I do when designing a book. One of the things that's so much fun about my job is that every book is different, so I never get bored and I always learn something new. Sometimes a book may be about a topic I think I'm not interested in at all. But pretty soon I get into the challenge. Sometimes I think it's even better in the end that I had an outsider's point of view on a subject.

I left my first job in publishing to go on to be a senior designer at another publisher, and after a couple of years I decided to start my own business. That first year at Knopf was the best possible way I could have started a career I love. As a designer, I've gotten to make my own illustrations for books, draw maps, make a lot of my own ornaments and typefaces, and even use a Xerox of my own face on a title page. Recently, I collaborated with my husband, Nick, who is a photographer, and used some of his work in a novel I designed. You never know if an author is going to like your vision of his or her book, so a large part of designing is knowing when to take a chance. Sometimes it works, and sometimes it doesn't. I now freelance for several publishers designing all kinds of books—children's books, cookbooks, books on baseball, golf, football, biographies of people as different as Jane Fonda and Coco Chanel. In the last seven years I've designed well over two hundred books. Needless to say, I need more bookshelves.

Claire Naylon Vaccaro holds a B.S. degree in graphic design from the State University of New York at Buffalo and a master's degree from Pratt Institute. She works in a studio she has set up in her sunlit loft in Manhattan's Soho district.

10

Blessed and Cursed

E L Y S E   D U B I N

From a very young age I've known one undeniable truth about myself. I am blessed and cursed with a peculiar mix of compulsive perfectionist and classic underachiever. What would I do with this combination? Surely it ruled out a lot of options—no eight years of medical school or five years of Ph.D. study for this poor soul. Of course, the concomitant insecurity gene that comes with the underachiever syndrome dictated that whatever profession I chose would have to be something marginally respectable yet certainly nothing that demanded too much in the way of hard preparation or laborious study. It would have to be something that came relatively naturally, something challenging and creative, and, perhaps above all, something intelligent. Something that I could divulge without embarrassment to a crowd at a cocktail party when the inevitable *"and what do you do?"* reared its ugly head. At the same time, and I say this sincerely, there would have to be an element of reward in it, a sense of somehow making a contribution to the world at large.

In retrospect, this character flaw has served me rather well. There's a certain privilege that comes with fessing up at a young age. At eight or nine, the child seemed precocious. Because I concentrated my energies on building dollhouses and drawing and painting at the kitchen table till the wee hours and writing daily girl-dream diary entries, my parents indulged my fancies with private art classes rather than the more conventional piano and dance lessons. I was later placed in what New York City's public schools called Talent Art, a program that worked a double period of art into my schedule every day, beginning in junior high and continuing through high school, and through that program I was awarded a scholarship to the Pratt Institute—a private fine arts college in Brooklyn, New York—an honor that I declined because I wanted to explore new territories in college, including all those new electives that were becoming the rage in the booming liberal arts— things like psychology, anthropology, and sociology. I'd been drawing and painting and batiking and sculpting for years, and I needed to know what else was out there.

I found those newfangled social sciences only mildly interesting, but I fell in love with literature. The professors were brilliant and passionate about their subjects, and the passion was contagious. The beauty of language coupled with the ideas of great minds inspired and awed me at once. I filled up on all the lit and poetry and drama and writing courses I could, even applied to a special program that waived all my distribution requirements so that I could take only English courses if I chose to, and I pretty much did just that. I was empowered by the notion that I could chart my own path. I didn't know exactly what I'd do with this made-to-order degree, but I felt satisfied that I was getting what I wanted out of college, and that made up for a lot of questions.

When I graduated with a degree in English, I felt the quiet panic that it would be as useless as it was rumored to be. But I chose to major in English not for vocation, after all, but because in my youthful, evolving view, writing and literature had meaning, somehow *mattered.* I wanted to go on reading. Reading was fun, not work, and felt like something entirely worthwhile *even while you were doing it,* which so much other college coursework did not seem—at least to me—and I dreaded the day that I would have to grow up and get a real job.

So I stalled by applying for a graduate fellowship, which would give me the opportunity to stay in school and stave off the real world a little longer, keep on reading, and, perhaps the biggest bonus, teach writing, which for me was the most exciting part. Fortunate for me, I got that fellowship and went to graduate school, but I spent that entire year knowing it would soon end and worrying about what would come next. What would I do when this second round of school was over? What would I do? I kept asking myself what it is that I love enough to spend my life doing. The answers kept coming to me in the same form. I love books, I love words, I love language, I love writing, I love art and design and all the things that I considered "creative." People would roll their eyes at that, and I understood. There was a romanticism to such a career wish list and no shortage of would-be writers and artists fresh out of college dreaming of the perfect "creative" job. Still, I kept coming back to the same things: books, words, language, writing, art, design. The one place where all those things converge is publishing, that much I knew, but where in the publishing machinery would they fit in, and how would I make a place for myself in it?

I read through the "Help Wanted" section of the Sunday *New York Times* trying to get a sense of what kinds of positions in publishing focused on those things. I had dreams of editing and designing and surrounding myself with others who loved writing and books and ideas; interestingly, I learned that most of the jobs that came closest to what I was imagining were jobs in production. I had little interest in sales or in contracts or in such material matters, or so I thought at the time. At some level I suppose I still feel that way—a true idealist never dies—but I have realized not just how hopelessly naive and idealistic such a view is but how important to the life and success of bookmaking in general those material matters really are.

I had picked up some experience in copyediting—that is, cleaning up and sometimes rewriting an author's manuscript submission as well as coding the design elements for the typesetter—by accepting a friend's generous offer to forward my résumé to her relative who was a publisher of scholarly books at Academic Press. I had no real publishing experience; I had taught writing for two years and knew my grammar, but that was a good start, it seemed. The publisher passed my résumé on to the man who was in charge of what they called editorial production, and he gave his time generously and helped to teach me the dos and don'ts of copyediting—what a good editor touches, avoids touching, must touch, and does not ever touch. I didn't agree with all his rules back then, but I am very glad that I had his good guidance. Private tutorials in editing are difficult to find if not unheard of, and I was very lucky. I learned from a pro. I have not yet met another person in publishing who had the good fortune of private coaching, although over the years I have tried to train my own staff in this same, personal, one-on-one style, but by no means is this kind of training a requisite for someone embarking on a career in editing.

After a few weeks of training assignments done at home and reviews of my progress in tutorial sessions, I began to copyedit book manuscripts at home for an hourly wage, known in the industry as freelance copyediting. Freelance copyediting is a service that almost all publishers of professional, reference, or nonfiction titles use. The authors of these manuscripts are specialists in a field—history, music, law, education, the sciences, medicine—they are not professional writers, so they usually both need and welcome someone's suggestions and (gentle) changes. This is also where a boring thing like mastering grammar comes in handy. If an editor makes a change, that editor had better know if that comma belongs in or out. Making arbitrary or inappropriate changes puts your very credibility as an editor on the line. It's bad enough if a book prints with typos and grammatical errors (and surely all do, to some extent, even when extreme care is taken—human error is inescapable) that were imposed by the author, but it's far worse if a book prints with errors imposed by you, the professional! Those two years I spent teaching English were the best editorial investment I ever made, as it turns out, because I really never knew the grammatical rules governing this language that I love until I had to teach them in college composition courses. So that's what a semicolon is really used for, I thought. A comma is not a "pause," for goodness' sake. I urge you to pick up a grammar book sometime. It can be quite an enlightening experience and one that you won't regret if you want to be a manuscript editor.

My first full-time job in publishing came in 1982 as a production editor for Pergamon Press, another scholarly/scientific publisher of books and journals. This scholarly/scientific angle was not really in my plan, and I was afraid, even at that very early stage in my career, of getting pigeonholed in a particular brand of publishing that was not my first choice. I had rather hoped to be doing something a bit more mainstream, but what I didn't realize then was that I would never have gotten this type of position at a bigger publisher. At large publishing houses nearly everyone at the entry level starts as an assistant. Bigger publishers are much more glamorous and easily attract eager young people. But at Pergamon I was doing what I truly wanted to be doing, and that was important to me. I was an editor with an independent workload and lots of autonomy. I could rewrite a professor's psychology article, design the typography of an entire book or journal (a skill in itself) in the typeface of my choosing, honor only those author corrections that I thought were meritorious and ignore those that seemed petty or insubstantial. By god, I thought, what a great job! There are few entry-level jobs that can be walked into with little hard experience that are simultaneously responsible, autonomous, creative, and interesting, and I had one! Mind you, this is not the most common path. It is much more usual to enter publishing as an editorial or production assistant, and there is much to be learned in those jobs. In fact, it is preferable to be taught well by someone who is knowledgeable than to flail around for years learning by trial and error, so if you have no training you'll appreciate and benefit from a good boss.

Many publishers, particularly small publishers and scientific, technical, and medical publishers, hire production editors with very little experience and cross their fingers that an intelligent, young, interested mind will learn quickly and well. Publishing is often a low-profit business and publishers want to fill jobs without spending a whole lot of money on the daily, routine matters of editing and production, but these jobs are the blood and guts of publishing. Production is where the whole raw mess begins and where the finished book is crafted. Everything from the design of the type, the design of the cover or jacket, the style of the prose, the amount of rewriting that needs to be done to the manuscript, how big the illustrations should be and where the legends should be positioned, communication with the author, and the later stages of typesetting, printing, binding—it all happens in production. Each title is like a child that needs to be shaped and nurtured, and after eight to twelve months of care and attention, it's off, often with your name mentioned somewhere in the acknowledgments, and will likely be kicking around in homes and on library shelves for years and years to come, even long after it is out of print, so there's a lot of incentive to do it right!

My first year in publishing was overwhelming and exhilarating and very, very frustrating. There was so much to learn, and so much work, and such tight schedules, that I honestly didn't know how I'd ever learn to juggle all the balls without dropping more than I caught. And of course, this was the challenge of it! I was assigned somewhere in the area of 14 journals—all in different subject areas: *Clinical Psychology Review, Annals of Tourism Research, Technology in Society, English for Specific Purposes,* and a host of others— some published quarterly, others bimonthly. It was my job to copyedit all the manuscripts myself; code all the design elements; send the manuscript to the typesetter and monitor the typesetter's schedules, quality of work, level of service, and pricing/billing; size artwork and control the quality of its production; send proofs to authors; troubleshoot for errors in the typeset pages and transfer the authors' corrections to the master set of page proofs; check that all the corrections were made properly when the revised page proofs came back from the typesetter; check over the mechanicals and paste up last-minute corrections on the final boards; coordinate advertising; send the issue to the printer; approve printer's proofs; quality control the printing; and keep all journals on schedule. Each journal issue had many contributors, and most of them needed to be chased by phone to get them to return their page proofs. The pace was fast and furious. I received more daily mail and packages than I could ever process, and found myself working until eight or nine o'clock trying to keep up. And so many details! I had notes taped everywhere reminding myself to make additional corrections that were phoned in late, or to check on a typesetting or printing job that was scheduled to be completed yesterday, or to change an author's affiliation, or to secure an ad to fill a blank page, or to add a coauthor's name to an article—the list is endless. After a few months I pleaded for permission to use freelance copy editors, and thankfully management was agreeable, so things improved a little. But just as I began to think I was gaining some real control over my workload, the book and journal departments merged and, unsurprisingly, I didn't lose any journals but I gained book projects. Two or three at first, which increased to five or six at a time in conjunction with the journal projects, and any hope of mastering my workload faded quickly.

I left that job after three crazy years, when a call from a publishing employment agency led me to Macmillan Publishing Company, where I accepted a job as editorial supervisor and went on to become managing editor of the reference division. But I am very grateful today for the madness of that first job at Pergamon. In addition to the many good friendships I took away with me, it prepared me for the worst and taught me perhaps the best lesson of all about the production side of this business: It will always be a high-pressure, frenzied, beat-the-clock place, and you must accept that as the nature of the beast, learn to live with it, and perhaps even thrive on the craziness. The object is to get the job done. You need to worry always about quality and price and schedule, but you have to know that even when it seems most unlikely, you will get the work done and, for the most part, get it done right. You learn to prioritize very quickly and well. Which job is running a week ahead of schedule? Any? Then let that sit if you must while you do this other thing that cannot wait. Which printer is more accommodating? If one will be more inclined to give you a rush schedule, use those favors and reward that supplier with more of your business or with extra time on another job. Communicate with all your freelancers and vendors. Get the author into the act; if his or her schedule permits, chances are the author will be glad to turn around proofs early, especially if it will mean books earlier. Juggle, juggle. It's the name of the game.

What you cannot afford in publishing is a bad job from any of the many fingers that touch each project. There is simply no time! In particular, a bad copyediting job will haunt a project and stall it every step of the way. A caution about copy editors—check their work! Until you are familiar with the particular idiosyncrasies of each of your freelancers, and they will each have their own, I guarantee it, it is critical that you monitor their work carefully. A copy editor who does too much rewriting, needless rewriting, will only enrage an author and is probably not paying attention to simple typos and bad grammar. I remember one copy editor who concentrated so much energy (erroneously) on spelling out numbers everywhere in a statistical manuscript that she missed most of the foreign-born author's simple agreement errors, and we wasted a lot of time and money in page proofs fixing the grammar of nearly every sentence in addition to having to restore all the spelled-out numbers to numerals. This is an editor's nightmare. The lesson: Quality control at every stage, particularly after copyediting is completed, and fix any problems before the manuscript is typeset.

Another good thing to always remember is that your suppliers are your allies, not your adversaries. Most young editors start out trying to bully their typesetters and printers (yes, I'm guilty, too): demanding better schedules, trying to pin the blame for a mistake on them, arguing about a bill, and so on. Do not fall into this trap. It's true, you have to keep your eyes open and be sure that you are getting what you pay for, that your schedules are being met, that your instructions are being carried out, and that a quality service is being provided, but always be fair and befriend your suppliers. If they are not doing the job, stop using them, but good suppliers are usually eager to help you out in a jam and will try to make informed decisions in good faith when working on your job. Their decisions might not always be the same ones you would make, but in publishing as in everything else, there's more than one acceptable way to do something and it's important to distinguish between acts of good faith and acts of negligence. A typesetter who sets a few headings in all caps because the type specifications that you sent were unclear is trying to do you a favor by not bothering you with a phone call. A typesetter who positions your artwork six pages after it was called out in the manuscript, even though the type specs say "position art immediately after callout," is careless. Rule of thumb: Be firm but fair, and treat others' mistakes with the same delicacy and diplomacy that you would want if the error were yours.

Perhaps the most challenging production project is the art book, that is, any book with a lot of illustration, especially color. The layout and design concerns can be mind-numbing in certain kinds of books, particularly textbooks or fancifully illustrated books. Each page, each spread, may present its own design problems. How big should the art be, or more likely, how big *can* it be if it has to be sized to fit on the same spread with the table and the bar chart and the text and the other elements? And when the design questions are resolved, many new ones take their place. Who will shoot your halftones? At what line screen will they reproduce best? What kind of paper will do them justice? Who will make your color separations? Strip your film? Where should the job be printed? Even after taking the best precautions for quality assurance, a wrong decision on any one of these questions can be the difference between a beautiful book and a washed-out, badly inked result. Printing is a complex process where any combination of paper, ink, water, or improper light exposure can ruin the finished product. Be sure to know which suppliers specialize in what you need. Ask production people at other publishers, call your suppliers for advice, and always get samples of a printer's recent work along with pricing. It's also important to keep in mind that a printed subject can only be as good as the original that you supply, so be sure that your criticism of the finished product is valid. It pays to inspect the original art upon submission and, when necessary, ask the author or the designer to get a more suitable replacement if possible.

A common question I hear from people interested in a career in publishing is, How does anyone live on the small salaries? It is true that publishing is not among the highest-paying professions—there is no denying that. As with anything, there are trade-offs. A sense of pride in what you do and integrity within the profession are big pluses. Coworkers are generally creative, intelligent people, and if they've been in the business for a while, odds are they have a good sense of humor. You have to when you fight deadlines daily. As for money, well, I'll say this. You can make money in publishing—not big money, but pretty respectable money. The trick is to learn your stuff, do it well, and move around a lot while you are making your way through the ranks. Stay with one company for two to three years, learn all you can, then look around for something at the next level. Call employment agencies that specialize in publishing and let them know you are interested in making a move. Sometimes a company will recognize your contribution with generous raises and promotions, but bigger salary jumps usually occur when you move to another company. As with everything, use your better judgment. If you love your job, factor that in; money is a poor substitute for an unsatisfying job. If big money is important to you, consider that publishing may not be for you. Truth is, most people in publishing are not in it for the money.

After over thirteen years in this business, I still feel like a kid at Christmas when those finished books arrive in my office for the first time. A new book in house is a hot-ticket item, and there are usually at least a few people who gather around to see and hold the new baby, occasionally a crowd. We rip open the boxes and there they are, hopefully more beautiful than we imagined, all those hundreds of pages of manuscript and photos and problems solved and schedules almost blown, wrapped neatly between two boards, looking very official and with no signs of distress. We congratulate each other, because it truly was a team effort and a labor of love, and after flipping through the crisp, newly printed pages and chatting about the book and smelling it (yes, smelling it—that just-off-the-presses, new-book smell), another title goes on the shelf. But there are new projects in production now with their own seemingly endless problems, and they beckon to us from our offices. And we are simultaneously drawn to them and over-whelmed by them. How will we ever get them done, we wonder. And as with all great loves, there is that well-celebrated love–hate dichotomy in this relationship, too, this relationship we have with our books, this publishing fever, this blessing and this curse.

Elyse Dubin received her undergraduate degree from Lehman College of the City University of New York, where she also attended graduate school. She has been in publishing for over thirteen years. She is currently associate director of production, adult trade division, for HarperCollins Publishers in New York.

11

Enter Indexer

SYDNEY WOLFE COHEN

All indexers seem to agree that no one begins book indexing with the intention of making it a career. Although I have met a few graduates from library school who claim to have prepared themselves for a life in indexing or abstracting, I remain convinced that indexing is one of those true Eureka professions. There is a meeting with yourself at an unexpected crossroads where various pathways of energy and ability, interest and skill and knowledge come together. For many on the road to the great Oz of, say, filmmaking, writing, or composing, this realization does not come right away. And the Eureka is not the Archimedes cry in discovering specific gravity. Rather, it is the subdued Eureka—my god, Eureka, I think this thing owns me.

I began indexing because a friend, an editor at Putnam, asked me one day if I would like to try indexing a book. Fortunately for me, I knew too little of the process to understand how much could go wrong in book indexing. My friend accepted the index with some minor changes. Apparently, things had gone right. Not bad for a first try. I had a new skill, and the next step was to exercise it. This meant sending out about a dozen letters with résumés to selected editors using my new IBM executive typewriter. When two or three editors called and asked me to visit their offices, I began to see where the next month's rent was coming from.

The word that came to mind then, however, was "stopgap." My plan was to use indexing to raise family income beyond the uncertain levels I achieved as a part-time teacher, part-time editor, and writer, at least until I could find a "real" job in publishing. Perhaps one of my indexing contacts might offer me a chance to work in-house. Stranger things had happened. I would not be the first freelancer whose work was rewarded with an editorial position. And was there a better way to find out which publishing environment suited my own temperament? Visiting publishing houses was both necessary as well as desirable.

Freelancers today might think it odd that in my early indexing days I personally picked up and returned indexing work. I did not use the postal service, UPS, messengers, or any other system of delivery available twenty-five years ago. (I don't think Fed Ex had yet taken wing from its creators' drawing boards.) In fact, I had only the sketchiest idea of how other indexers worked, since I had never met another indexer, nor was I to meet one until I had been indexing for at least eight years. Besides, I rarely kept a copy of my indexes, and I hated the idea of entrusting an index manuscript to a stranger after all the work that had gone into the manuscript—four pages or four hundred pages, it did not matter. And speaking of work, that subterranean life of the freelancer—as appealing as I sometimes found it—required occasional relief. Getting out of the house and into the social fluorescence of the publishing office was part of the price of sanity.

An indexer's work, postpone it as one may, usually takes possession of one's life soon after the first day. Whatever the merits of the book, I could not escape an involvement in the author's mind and material, which often relegates to a distant second place many of the personal responsibilities, passions, and daily must-dos that usually preoccupy one's thoughts.

I would often sit at my desk, still in my bathrobe, coffee cup at my elbow, cigarette mounds rising in the ashtray as the hands of my wall clock spun around, listening to radio music with hourly news intervals flashing by, until the night had come and almost gone, not satisfied until I had approximated the elusively ideal index for the book at hand. I ended my work with the feeling that I knew the book better than anyone ever would, sometimes including the author. "Ask me anything you want to know about the cave paintings of the Upper Adige," I might ask a friend after indexing a book on that subject, "at least for the next week while I remember it."

The author was not the person I would be taking my finished index to. Although authors almost always pay for the index out of their royalties, indexers and authors rarely meet or speak, which is probably just as well. They both have strong emotional links to the same infant. It would be years before I met an author, a book editor, a project editor, had lunch with a senior copy editor, years before I met other freelancers. It was a revelation when I attended my first meeting of the American Indexing Society and found an entire hotel room filled with other indexers. It was like discovering a branch of my family that I never knew existed. Talk about networking. Today indexers and other freelancers quickly learn that success in publishing is gained not by isolated forays but in learning from each other at meetings, in classrooms, and sharing information through newsletters. Whatever I learned in that first year, I learned from trial and error or from the copy chiefs and production editors with whom I worked.

The production editor, sometimes the senior copy editor, is the go-between, and this is the person to whom I would deliver my work, happy to have a reason to shave, get into a suit, and visit the electric publishing world in midtown Manhattan. Whatever success, whatever joy there was in my life as an indexer, I would soon learn, depended on the quality of my relationship with the production editor. He, or more often she, was the only person in publishing, outside of the receptionist, with whom I had more than casual contact.

Meeting one of the first production editors for whom I would work was better luck than I knew at the time. Ed Doremus was a respecter of detail who ran the production machinery at T. Y. Crowell until that long-established, independent company was swallowed whole by Harper. He then stayed on to help his counterpart there, Dolores Simon, with the added books and people involved in the corporate digestion process. Ed rarely missed an opportunity to comment on my indexes, usually in a phone call on the morning after I turned in the manuscript.

"In subheadings when one preposition follows another," he might say, "as in 'policy role of in Truman administration,' shouldn't you use a comma to separate the prepositions?" As an evening school English teacher, I would improvise a somewhat arcane rule governing the grammatical exceptions applicable to index subentries. "Indexing subs are not governed by ordinary rules of syntax," I might say.

Ed would respond with "Hmm. I'll have to think that over." And I would hang up, realizing that I would have to think it over as well. Without anyone saying any more about it, a reader of my next index for Ed would find a comma between every pair of prepositions in subentries.

More likely, there would be no double prepositions at all. What I eventually learned was more than the fact that index structures were not exempt from grammatical law. I learned that indexes were not the best vehicles for grammatical subtleties, defendable or not.

As in politics, the appearance of error was as bad as error itself. It was better to avoid indexing structures that made an editor look cross-eyed at an entry and wonder what might be wrong with it.

During my first year, I was also learning the professional dimensions of my work, thanks to Ed and a few other editors who took the indexing process as seriously as they did other aspects of book publishing. There was nothing in an index that did not deserve at least as much thought as the text of the book itself. I began to see the index as the most compressed, complex, and necessary chapter of a nonfiction book. And an indexer had to be prepared to explain why any specific entry, or lack thereof, was the best choice for the index. I was finding out that the first obligation of a professional was to diminish the anxieties of his clients rather than add mystery to their lives.

When I arrived at the reception desk in those first months of indexing, I wasn't yet aware of another lesson I was learning. A publishing house is much more than the voice of a production editor on the phone. Each publishing company is a distinctly individual tribe with its own way of dealing with the power, reality, and magic of book production. In visiting an editorial office I would learn something about its social setting, its "corporate culture." It mattered if I discovered that a given publishing house was a well-regimented army following orders from above or a pressure cooker of steaming editorial relationships, where commands were bellowed from one tense cubbyhole office to the next. Once after completing my assignment I arrived at a publisher in time to see the managing editor storm out of one of the offices that surrounded a general work area, complaining loudly that she was sick and tired of all the mistakes that were getting into the final page proofs of her books. For emphasis she converted her pen into a javelin and flung it into the corkboard wall across the room. It helped to know about the emotional climate of the people who were assigning work to me. I was able to figure their needs when I called to negotiate for more time and/or space to do my index.

Visits to another company, which specialized in thick books on law and finance, provided less stimulating experiences. I needed the usually long wait in the library—a quiet and dimly lit reception area—to prepare for my entrance into the main editorial office, a single large room with rows of men in white shirts reading, marking, shuffling, staring at stacks of pages with the reverential attention one might expect in a banking firm. Surely, it took a different kind of person to work in this atmosphere.

Publishing has a niche for nearly everyone, and I was finding that my own role just might be that of a visitor from my own private space. Freelancing gave me the opportunity to work alone, which I liked, and still have just the right amount of contact with the in-house people with whom I was beginning to form long-term business friendships based not only on mutual trust and cooperation but also on the kind of affection that can often flourish among people who work a little distance from each other. And so a day came a few years later where I admitted to myself that my career was settled. I was a freelance indexer.

I rarely make house calls these days, and when I do it is likely to be a social call rather than an appearance as a visiting indexer. And the irony is that I don't work alone anymore, because as my work grew I had to take on assistants, develop my own staff, and preside over the evolution of my own corporate culture. I learned my lessons well and ended up by making an in-house job for myself, which is, after all, what I was looking for in that first year in publishing. The only problem is that I miss the freedom I had then, before I learned so much.

Sydney Wolfe Cohen studied English literature at New York University and Columbia, taught at the City University of New York, C. W. Post, and Rutgers, and is presently adjunct assistant professor of publishing at NYU and CEO of S. W. Cohen and Associates, an indexing service.

12

What Is a Cash Cow, Anyway?

 T H O M A S S . N O V A K

It was spring of 1980 when I first got a phone call from David Godine. I had been in Boston for a year and a half, was working for a midsize energy and environmental consulting firm, and was looking to change jobs and run the business side of a small company offering a service or product in which I believed. I had worked for several small arts organizations since college, was searching for a match of my skills and interests, and working for a book publisher sounded promising.

The Godine office at the time was in the basement of the Ames Webster mansion in Boston's Back Bay. Actually, it was more garden level than basement and consisted of two large, open rooms and a few smaller ones housing a staff of ten. I was immediately intrigued by David and his books. The company had been in business eleven years, and David made it clear that the business manager's position was very difficult and demanding, an all-consuming job, possibly the worst in the company. Money was tight, the company was undercapitalized and growing, the pressures would be constant, but I would learn a lot about publishing very quickly. After a second interview with David, I met the chairman of his board (who was also the chairman of a midsize downtown bank), and when the job was offered, I took it.

I received only two days of training since the interim business manager that summer was eager for some vacation before heading back to Harvard Business School for her second year. Two days was not nearly enough time to go over all that needed to be covered, even though my predecessor did leave very detailed notes of procedures. So I was thrown to the wolves, basically learning on the job.

It was clear to me that everyone wears many hats in a small business. Among my responsibilities were cash management (at the top of the list), accounts payable and receivable, budgeting, planning, royalty reporting, preparing financial statements, overseeing the warehousing and filling of orders for books, and coordinating an annual audit. At the time, we did our own invoicing (through a service bureau) and customer service, while subcontracting out the picking, packing, and shipping of the books. Filling our own orders meant billing customers directly and doing our own collections, a tough assignment for any small publisher. Interest rates were high, independent booksellers were strapped for cash, and we were much too small to have any collection clout. As a result, cash was always tight and cash flow unpredictable, which made it very difficult to make and keep commitments to authors and suppliers. Requests for payment were constant and came from all directions—the payroll and taxes had to be paid, royalty advance money was needed to sign up new books, freelance designers had to be paid quickly or we'd lose them, suppliers (primarily paper merchants, printers, and binders) needed to be kept happy so they would continue taking on new work, authors were owed royalties, and the bank did not want us overdrawing our account. Every dollar had to be spent wisely.

Cash flow dominated my life that first year. When making collection calls to independent booksellers, I was often reassured that they loved Godine books and admired the publishing program, but they had to pay Random House, Simon & Schuster, Norton, Harper, Oxford, Putnam, Houghton Mifflin, and others before paying Godine. We were at the top of very few lists. It was not unusual to get paid 150 to 180 days after the invoice date, yet our vendors did not want to wait 180 days before being paid by us. Being new to the book business, I was amazed (I now know naively) to learn that not only could booksellers dodge bills for many months, but they could then "pay" these bills by returning unsold books for full credit. Because of our ongoing cash needs, our relationship with booksellers was somewhat confrontational at times. Occasionally, we would put a bookstore on credit hold, but the truth was (and still is) that booksellers could easily get Godine books from wholesalers if their credit with them was good, so credit hold from any publisher, large or small, is essentially more bark than bite. There is always a way for booksellers to get the books they want.

The flip side to collecting money is owing money. Every day the phones rang with suppliers looking to be paid for work they had done months ago. And my colleagues on the staff lobbied me to pay their folks first—editors for authors, the managing editor for freelance copy editors and proofreaders, the marketing folks for advertisers, and so forth. Sometimes I felt overwhelmed prioritizing who should get paid first and who should be delayed, so I initiated a monthly meeting of the senior staff during which we decided as a group the priorities for that month. But without a healthy or dependable cash flow, it was impossible to keep everyone happy. I tried paying a little something to most everyone every month and did not make commitments I could not keep. I preferred being honest up front rather than being optimistic and finding later we couldn't pay what we had promised. Printing and paper reps often stopped by when they were in the neighborhood to see me (and David), hoping to walk away with a check. Needless to say, a fair amount of tension was involved in owing so many people overdue money, so I tried to ease the anxiety with a little comic relief: "Tell me a good joke, and I'll write you a check," I offered. Not everyone appreciated this approach, but many knew that if they had a good joke, they'd get a check. It may not have been for the full amount owed, but it was something. (I built a contingency into each month's allocation of cash for exceptional jokes!) Vendors often called and, without even identifying themselves, would begin telling me their jokes. It brought a breath of fresh air to an otherwise stressful situation. And I heard and shared a lot of terrific jokes.

In addition to managing the cash, providing timely and accurate information to my coworkers was an important part of my job. For instance, units and dollars of sales, returns (of unsold books), cost of goods sold (both manufacturing and royalty), subsidiary rights income, operating expenses, cash on hand, receivables, inventory levels, payables, debt—all this information needed to be gathered, assembled, and reported to David and the senior staff so we knew where we stood and could make informed decisions. Since we were just beginning to computerize, most of this data was decentralized in manual ledgers that needed to be summarized and presented in a format that made sense and was useful to the staff.

Since the daily management of the business department was so consuming, it was nearly impossible to find the time to step back from the day-to-day activities to do the necessary planning for the future. The company was growing 30 to 40 percent a year, and there just wasn't enough time or support to do everything that should have been done. Putting out the daily fires (which usually meant calming irritated suppliers or authors who were owed money) clearly took precedence over planning for the future, and this was a source of real frustration for me.

It eventually became clear that not only would I lose all my hair if we didn't get out of the collections business, but the survival of the company would soon be at risk. Everyone (including David) spent far too much time wrestling with the many problems of being cash poor. We had to do something radically different if we were to stay in business and grow. So we explored distribution (and sales representation) with larger publishing houses and settled on Harper & Row. This company had both feet in the client service business and serviced many presses our size. Visions of a predictable cash flow, minimal bad debt, and staff time freed up from collections fueled what proved to be a good decision. Less staff time was spent on collection issues and much more on editorial and marketing matters. Getting out of the collections business allowed me more time to provide up-to-date, accurate information to my coworkers, track trends, and begin planning for the future. The Harper sales force was calling on more accounts than our commission reps did, and sales were growing. (Commission reps sell books for many smaller publishers, nonexclusively.) The downside was that Harper was publishing three lists a year instead of two so we were constantly battling list deadlines, and we had to follow the Harper fulfillment policies instead of setting our own.

In the early 1980s, David was a media darling. He was often called upon to give the small-press perspective in a big-press world. Several reviews of Godine books on the front page of the *New York Times Book Review* brought the company tremendous visibility. Yet even with all the breaks, we always seemed behind the eight ball. A front-page review certainly increased sales, but never enough to get out from under the weight of our debts. Perhaps we weren't maximizing our good fortune and opportunities. Maybe we were trying to do too much too quickly. We were rapidly growing on margins that were very slim, and there was simply not enough capital to support the growth.

Life at a smaller publisher is a bit like a ride on a roller coaster: The highs and lows are punctuated by intermittent bouts of nausea. Some small companies manage to ascend from the low points and hang on for another ride; unfortunately, others, such as the distinguished North Point Press, are no longer riding the roller coaster.

Working with the staff at Godine was a fabulous experience. My colleagues were (mostly) young, smart, energetic, hardworking, enthusiastic, and scrappy. It sometimes seemed like graduate school, except we were publishing real books in the real world. Something about the uphill battles we faced as a small, Boston-based publisher brought us together more as family than merely as coworkers. Being poor will do that, I guess. David had a knack for attracting talent, and we were all given a lot of freedom to do our jobs. It wasn't apparent then, but it's clear to me now, that success at a small publishing house is the result of having not only very good books but also a talented staff working harmoniously toward common goals.

I learned an enormous amount about publishing and running a small business that first year. I learned that trade publishing, where culture intersects with commerce, is a very risky business, one with terribly slim margins, especially when production quality (Godine's trademark), and therefore production costs, are high. I learned that publishing and bookselling are no longer hobbies for the genteel bibliophile. Those days are over. To survive, both have to be run as businesses. I learned that bookselling is basically a consignment business, although no publisher likes to call it such, and most books need to be sold twice, first to the bookseller in order to be shelved and then to the individual customer. Every book needs its own marketing strategy, and what works successfully for one may not work well on a similar book. Unlike most industries, publishers often compete directly with their primary distribution agents, the booksellers, by trying to reach the consumers through direct mail, catalog sales, or special sales. This is often a source of irritation with booksellers, but publishers are trying to sell as many copies of every book as possible. I learned that one role small publishers play is discovering new voices, and then often losing those voices to larger publishers with deeper pockets. But I also learned that those who choose to work in book publishing are hardworking, smart, interesting, talented people who are devoted to books, and that alone can make all the hard work worthwile.

Thomas S. Novak graduated from the State University of New York at Buffalo in 1975 with a B.S. in business administration. He spent four years as the business manager of David R. Godine, Publisher, Inc. and remains a friend and adviser to David and his company. Tom has been the chief financial officer at Beacon Press for the past eight years.

13

Willing to Be Lucky

 KRISTIN KLIEMANN

I was staying in deepest Brooklyn, and the *"subway"* was above ground—deeply baffling to me on my first day in New York. Also baffling was the fact that after I bought my token, I met with tremendous resistance from the turnstile. I continued to slam myself against the stubborn metal bar (token held high in my left hand), thinking that if only I could get in there and on the train, I would gladly hand my token over to the conductor who, I was certain, was strolling the aisles greeting all the riders by name! (Who knows why I thought New York was like that scene in *Meet Me in St. Louis*; too many movies and too few cities in my youth!) I may have known my way around a business letter, but I sure didn't have a clue about New York. Much of the next year (my first year, I thought my only year) was spent getting to know not just Publishing but this big fat hot dirty *inspiring* city. (And for those of you who don't already know it, here's some advice: *Do* put that token in the little slot in the turnstile. The bruise from my little adventure lasted at least three days!)

When I arrived in New York in August of 1979, I had a few basic skills that would serve me well in looking for my first "real" publishing job: I could type at least forty words per minute, and I knew what a business letter was supposed to look like. (Oh yes, I knew my way around an IBM Selectric. I could set my margins, knew how to type "Dear First Name" and double-space the body, and close with a centered signature block and put in that lovely bit at the end with my boss's initials in caps and mine after the colon in lowercase.)

In addition, I'd worked in offices before (even if it was only part-time for a dermatologist, or two hours a week for the chairman of the history department in college), so I knew what to do with the hold button on my phone: "Oh, Boss, there's a woman on the phone, but she says she's Mr. Big-wig's office. Would you like to talk to Mr. Big-wig's office?" And I knew how to organize an appointment schedule, remain cheerful in the face of the drudgery of filing and calm in the face of pressure to get things done quickly; I even stayed late at the dermatologist's office to alphabetize the drug company samples.

I had also "studied" publishing during my senior year in college, writing letters to people in the field, reading books by and about great editors, and I'd worked on the literary magazine, which meant at least two trips to the printer with proofs I'd read and mechanicals I'd pasted myself.

And then there were the four weeks of the Summer Publishing Program at Rice University in Houston: day after day, lecture after lecture by real live publishing professionals, each more interesting and more glamorous than the next, and each so clearly in love with his or her job.

It was because of this publishing program that I decided to come to New York. I'd been accepted into an M.F.A. program for the fall, but I now deferred entrance for a year in order to go to New York. I was certain one year was plenty of time to learn all I'd need to know (all there was to know) about publishing. And after that year, I'd return to my life as a poet, with an eye on eventually moving back to Texas to start a publishing company of my own. I'd publish poets. And within a decade I'd be famous and revered as the woman who'd brought the world another generation of greats.

After the publishing program, I spent a month looking for temporary jobs, saving money, and writing letters (perfectly typed, of course) to everyone who'd spoken at the program:

> Dear So-and-so:
> Your lecture on _____ was so fascinating that I've decided to come to New York and become a _____ just like you. Here's my résumé. Would you have time to meet with me during the first week in August? And even if you don't have a position open in your area of the company, would you mind passing the résumé along to someone else who might be willing to see/hire an eager beaver like me?
>
> Cheerfully yours,

By August first I'd saved enough for a one-way plane ticket, and I took advantage of a promise from an ex-boyfriend's college roommate, who now lived in Brooklyn and agreed (heaven knows why) to pick me up at La Guardia and let me stay for a week *until I found a job.*

That's how it was: not *if* I found a job, but *when.* I just knew it would happen. My conviction stemmed mainly from the fact that I was willing to take whatever job came my way! So off I went on my interviews.

Of course, every job proved to be every bit as interesting as I had expected. I took typing tests, talked to personnel officers, and quickly learned that department heads in the other-than-editorial departments were delighted to be meeting any young person who was willing to allow that perhaps the life of an editor wasn't the only goal worth striving for. So I began to tell people upon first introduction that I thought the money side, the sales and marketing side, was beginning to sound like the road for me. And I meant it.

This led to an interview with a woman who had just started as a subsidiary rights manager at Harcourt Brace Jovanovich. My résumé began with the following line: "Personal Statistics: Single, 22, healthy." (I'd read in a book, one of those "how to write a winning résumé" books, that this was an appropriate way to begin. As you can see, I had a few things to learn about writing résumés, not to mention equal opportunity.) Anyway, the interview began with her amused grin and the comment, "Well, I'm glad you're healthy!" We talked for at least forty-five minutes, and as I was getting ready to leave, she said, "Don't you want to know what the position pays?" To which I replied cheerfully, "Oh no, I'm sure it doesn't pay much at all. We were told at the publishing program that entry-level jobs in book publishing pay just over poverty wages."

Three days later, I was offered a job by a literary agent, but I was still stuck on the idea that I had only one year to learn all there was to know about publishing. And I thought I'd be better off *in* a publishing house than outside at an agency. So I decided to call the subsidiary rights manager at Harcourt Brace to see if she liked me as much as I liked her.

It was Friday. By now, I was getting down to the last of my money, and Thursday night's call to my parents (from a pay phone on the street in the rain) had ended with my mother very sweetly saying to me that I could come home next week if I hadn't found anything, at which point my father came on the phone and said, less sweetly, that he hoped I'd now proven to myself whatever it was I'd set out to prove and that he hoped I'd have the good sense to "come in out of the rain and get your bucket home where it belongs!" Dad was a bit stressed by the idea of his eldest, a daughter who very much resembled him, hitting the big city. Looking back, I can't say I blame him—after all, I *was* standing in the rain.

My week in Brooklyn had ended, and I was now staying with a friend from college who was in the process of renovating a fourth-floor walk-up in "alphabet city." We'd been eating plaster dust in the ninety-degree heat and 100 percent humidity all morning, when I decided to walk over to the nearest pay phone and make my call to Harcourt Brace. As I crossed Fourteenth Street and Avenue A, I realized that a call from the street might sound less than professional, so I decided to use one of the pay phones in the back of the post office. I was hot and dirty, wearing ratty old clothes, and when a character in front of the bodega just this side of the post office began to speak to me about his deepest fantasies for the two of us together, I knew enough not to be shocked by, or interested in, what he had to say. I entered the cool of the post office and headed for the phones. As I dialed the number and looked to my right, I realized that the street man had followed me in and was now standing some ten feet away with his hand active in his pocket, still chanting about the lovely life that could be ours.

I panicked when the ring was answered on the other end by the very woman for whom I dearly wanted to work! Our conversation went something like this:

What we said	What was rushing through my mind
Me: Hello, this is K-Mumble, K-Mumble.	*I don't want him to hear my name!*
She: Who? Oh yes, the healthy one!	
Me: Have you made a decision yet? I mean, I've been offered another job.	*Oh no, he's still listening. What am I saying to her? What is he doing in that pocket?*
She: Well . . .	
Me: Listen, I'd really like to work for you! I'll do anything!	*What am I saying? I'll do anything? Would that include staying in this big fat hot dirty and maybe not-so-inspiring city filled with perverts who have no fear of the U.S. postal authorities?*
She: Well . . .	
Me: How about if I started Monday? [Giggle.] What time would you like me to be there?	*What am I doing? Do I even want to spend one more minute, much less one whole year, in this disgusting place? What is he doing now?*

Somehow my new boss and I came to an agreement, and I sped out of that post office and back to the dust-filled apartment of my friend vowing that whatever happened, I would *never* tell my father about any of this.

It is now fifteen years later. Within a month of starting that first job, I was sure I had happened upon the greatest job in publishing ever! And since I'm now a director of subsidiary rights, whose assistant is just halfway through *her* first year in publishing, I suppose I have a vested interest in explaining, if only to her, why I was correct in believing that being a subsidiary rights assistant is, indeed, a great job.

I must confess that I spend part of nearly every day thinking about, referring back to, and relying on what I learned during that first year. While all entry-level jobs in publishing do to a certain extent require the same skills and lead to learning some of the same methodology and publishing protocol, what is particularly satisfying about being in a rights department is that by the very nature of the work you are exposed to a wide variety of in-house people, as well as to a large number of publishing types from other companies: paperback publishers, book club administrators, magazine editors, editors from foreign publishers, audiocassette publishers, story editors—the list is endless.

The work, too, is endless. But that's a boon for someone like me with the attention span of a flea: I am, believe it or not, completely justified in starting my day by thinking about whether or not Book-of-the-Month Club and *Parade Magazine* will be interested in a book that outlines the complete history of the hamburger. Moreover, after a whole day of pursuing any number of unrelated, completely fascinating possible deals, I might end my day by contemplating how the appearance of a Portuguese-language edition of Ross Perot's books might affect both the world political scene and my own monthly record of subsidiary rights income.

Of course, early on, the lofty thoughts of what to sell where (or at least what to pitch where) were left to my new boss at Harcourt Brace Jovanovich. Mine was not to wonder why—mine was to serve and learn, learn, learn. From the moment I opened (and read!) all the mail in the morning to the moment I finished filing the last bit of paper at the end of the day, I was a veritable sponge for publishing "juice." My responsibilities provided me the opportunity to learn a variety of important lessons. The following are a few examples.

By having to answer the phone in an efficient and professional fashion, I had contact with a veritable who's who of the publishing world, which meant I knew at least a bit about who to call for what, when I got my second job.

Gathering the necessary back-up material needed to respond to the questions in that day's mail gave me a what's what for various types of subsidiary rights deals, which taught me how deals were made in terms of money, contracts, and the complicated problems that nearly always arise.

Having to gather and photocopy reviews, sales information, printing information, etc., as backup to submissions my boss would make showed me that excellent skills at the copy machine cannot be stressed too much. One must learn exactly how to tape up a torn newspaper review in such a way that the feeder mechanism will not eat the review *and* all seventeen copies will be completely legible.

Organizing meetings and lunches on my boss's calendar, making lunch reservations, and doing expense reports meant talking to all the other assistants in other departments (my first friends in publishing!). Lunch is an important part of publishing, too.

Alphabetizing the books on my boss's bookshelf—In this particular instance I think I learned that assistantship can be obsessive.

As time went on (I stayed at this job for just under two years), I was awarded responsibilities that afforded me greater independence and greater exposure. I began to coordinate all the subsidiary rights deals involving the production department. (We would often print copies for a British publisher, which meant I handled trafficking of their required changes, saw to it that their books were shipped and billed on time, etc.) And I clearly remember negotiating my first deal: a license for newspaper syndication rights to *The Burning Bed* by Faith McNulty, which was later made into a TV movie that served as a vehicle for Farrah Fawcett to prove her ability as a serious actress. My syndication deal was a result of an auction that ran over two or three days and was probably the single moment of that first year that made me realize (a) that this was a lot of fun! and (b) that I'd never learn it all in one year!

I must also say that one of the reasons I think often about that first year is that I learned one hundred lessons about what constitutes being a good boss and what to strive for in creating an efficient and inspired rights department. I had the good fortune of blundering into a job working for a woman who not only really knew her stuff but wanted me to learn as much as I possibly could. And, in general, that whole department (there were five or six of us at different times over the year) was set up to allow each of us as broad a range of experiences as we were able to handle. Let me also say that there were lessons learned negatively, experiences that fell into the category of "When I grow up and run the world, I won't make the same mistakes I'm witnessing here! Harrumph! Harrumph!" For the most part, I probably don't make those same mistakes; however, I'm sure I've created my own special variety of grievous errors in judgment. (Which of course does not stop me from still saying today, "When I grow up, I won't make the same mistakes, etc., etc.")

Perhaps the best thing I can say about the years I've spent so far in this business is that it would be equally possible for me to contemplate the writing of an essay entitled "What I Learned During My Second Year" or "What I Learned in My Tenth Year," or heaven knows, I could say quite a bit about the past two years I've spent here at Hyperion/Disney Press, learning exactly how a new publishing house starts from ground zero. And while it seems unlikely at this point that I will ever return to Texas or start my own publishing adventure devoted exclusively to poetry, I've made a certain peace with working in New York City. E. B. White said, "No one should come to New York unless he is willing to be lucky." And lucky I have been!

Kristin Kliemann has a B.A. in English and sociology from Trinity University in San Antonoio, Texas. After eighteen months in her first job at Harcourt Brace Jovanovich, she left to join the rights department at Farrar, Straus & Giroux. After ten years at FSG, she left for her current job as the subsidiary rights director for Hyperion/Disney Press. Kris teaches in the publishing program at New York University and lives in Hastings-on-Hudson, New York with her husband and son.

14

Dancing School

MARYANN PALUMBO

In this era of television and video, reading is still the only way I can totally escape from the real world. I majored in English at Brooklyn College, where sometimes I was required to read fifteen books at once. I loved it. As a child I spent a lot of time at the library each week taking out the maximum four books allowed. At the beginning of the summer my local library allowed me to check out as many books as I liked. The day after school ended, I would go to the library and check out as many as thirty books. I would take a book to my room and spend at least three or four hours each morning reading until my mother would summon me to breakfast. One chapter later, I would make my entrance at the breakfast table. I had a similar routine at night, reading until my mother would call out, "Is that light still on?" Reading was my most pleasurable activity. It was my vacation. This was the way I traveled, met people, experienced relationships, escaped my shyness, cried, and laughed. Reading was the most important and rewarding thing I did.

I was a voracious reader, but it never occurred to me that I could ever make a living in the book business. My publishing career began as an accident. However, the book fairy was watching out for me. An uncle who worked in the printing business told me about an opening he had heard about in book publishing. I was offered the job and took it. This first job in publishing was an entry-level position as secretary to the vice president of sales at World Publishing Company. My responsibilities included general secretarial duties: typing, filing, answering the phones, taking dictation. I liked my boss, my colleagues, and basically enjoyed what I was doing. But the job never kept me busy enough, so I volunteered to help other colleagues in the sales department. As it turned out, volunteering became the pivotal decision of my working life.

By volunteering, I changed a clerical job into a publishing career. Making personal phone calls, arranging my paper clips, and staring into space just wasn't a satisfying way to spend my day, so I leaned over and asked a colleague in front of me if there was any work I could help her with. She was surprised, and when she recovered she said, "Sure. I'm drowning and could use some help." I paid attention to her instructions and followed them accurately and when I was finished, presented her with my results. She was delighted, and whenever time permitted, I volunteered to help again. I learned that taking the initiative, paying attention to the task at hand, and doing the job asked was the way to make people feel confident in you, know that you are a team player, and want to share information with you.

World allowed me to roll up my sleeves and try everything. Whenever I wasn't typing or answering the phone, I was planning and attending sales conferences, helping to create promotional materials, interacting with the sales force, and—all the while— soaking up as much experience as possible. Suddenly I was invited to attend meetings where I began to absorb information that I still find useful today. At a cover concept art meeting, I learned that while there are a number of primary colors, some colors sell more of a product than others. Blue is a cool color, and red is a warm color that actually has been proven to sell more products. World published a brand-new dictionary and used a red cover, which became a huge success. Twenty-five years later, I'm still going to cover meetings, and red covers still outsell blue covers.

I worked as many hours as it took to get a job done. This was a very important lesson for me. When you're learning, time is irrelevant. This is a critical period to soak up as much experience as possible. Watching the clock won't help you learn anything. A key lesson that I learned that first year was to forget about the clock! Five o'clock meant nothing. In no time the job took over me. I loved everything about it. I couldn't work harder, or longer hours. Every minute was fun.

Then disaster struck—my boss quit. Suddenly I worried about not having a position in the company. I didn't know if a new boss would be brought in. Would he like me? Would he keep me? It never occurred to me that my volunteering had paid off. Much to my surprise, I learned I was an important part of the sales team. I was needed and valued by the staff whether I had a boss or not. I was asked to stay on. I was thrilled and continued my hard work, again volunteering whenever I could—until another disaster struck. World was going through a tumultuous time of upper-management struggle. Suddenly there were resignations, confusion, and a period of instability. Half of the sales department left. Again much to my surprise, the former trade sales manager of World called and offered me a job with a generous increase in salary at the new publishing company, Intext Press, he'd recently joined as vice president of sales. I jumped at the opportunity. I had no idea this man even knew who I was. Much later when I asked him why he offered this position to me, he replied it was because I had shown initiative, enthusiasm, and wasn't averse to working long hours. I became assistant to the vice president of sales at Intext Press.

Intext was a much smaller publisher. In this environment I was able to learn about the entire publishing process, which took me way beyond my area of sales administration. In a larger company you often tend to be pigeonholed in one area instead of learning the whole process. As usual, I was not satisfied with the restrictions of my everyday duties. Pretty soon I was asking lots of questions and getting some disappointing answers. Although the smaller company gave me more opportunities for growth, it had a smaller staff and fewer resources. I desperately needed resources, so I took up the challenge of creating my own. I realized this company didn't have a complete catalog that listed and annotated every single book it published. This was inconceivable to me. At World, we had many catalogs. At Intext we had virtually none.

I made the suggestion that I could create an annotated catalog of every single title published by the company. My boss gave me carte blanche to proceed with the project as long as I got my other work done. I knew he was pessimistic about my ability to take on such a daunting project alone. But I knew I could do it. This was just the challenge I needed. And so I spent the next six months in a dusty old library reading and writing catalog copy on every single book the company offered for sale. Here at last was my own project. It was my idea, my execution, my determination—and my skin if it didn't work. The catalog was the first independent experience of my career, and it amounted to hundreds of hours and titles to cover. My determination far exceeded my good sense. Finally I produced this enormous marketing tool, which I proudly presented to my boss. He was flabbergasted. He couldn't believe I had done this. He showed it to the president, who applauded and encouraged me to complete the project. My boss told me that now that I had finished the catalog, I needed to get it printed at a reasonable cost.

Remember that uncle who first got me into this mess? As the only printer I knew, he was the one I called to rescue me! Not only did he find me my first job, I now begged him to quote (give me a cost estimate) on printing this project and hoped it would be a fair price. Of course, I had no idea of what a fair price would be. This was my first experience with outside contractors. When my uncle came back with his quote, I was told that people thought his prices were too high. I was embarrassed. Colleagues gave me the names of two other printers who would submit quotes (prices) for the same job. Bless you, Uncle John. You came in with the best price. In dealing with outside contractors, I learned that each bidder did not offer the same service. I learned about the quality of paper, typefaces, types of binding, weight of the catalog, and much more. (Many years later, I still find myself negotiating for good quality at a fair price.) My uncle got the job, I got a promotion, and the company now had an invaluable sales and marketing tool.

Suddenly my boss had come to rely on me for ideas and suggestions, and the rest of the company realized the same. And suddenly I knew marketing was the career for me. I loved creating ideas and materials to help sell books, working with and promoting authors, and seeing the satisfying results. I was now sales promotion coordinator. I was given my own responsibilities including working in sales as well as promotion and publicity. I now dealt directly with the sales force. I sent them their weekly mailings, calculated their commissions, created and sent them the marketing materials they needed. It seemed clear to me that marketing was my future. I was given free rein to do everything from tracking books from production to their warehouse ship dates to the bookstores, to interacting with other departments such as editorial, subsidiary rights, accounting, order processing, production, and the art department.

As a child, I was extremely shy. My mother's solution to this problem was to take me to dancing school, where I learned to dance in a group of other children. We learned to dance in sync and behave as a team. Many years later this interaction reappeared in my business world. I learned I had to be in sync with other people and departments—to be a team player—to get the job done. I learned in the business world that you have to work with other people, understand what they do and how that affects what you do. I learned not to be embarrassed by asking for help, because people love to tell you what they know, and so I love to share with people what I know.

By now I knew marketing was the area in which I excelled and which I enjoyed the most. While I was so immersed in all this creativity, my boss was fired! A new guy was brought in who didn't have experience in my area of publishing. At first I was anxious. I thought he wouldn't keep me. But I was astonished when he asked me to help him understand an area of the business that I understood better than he did. Other colleagues had told him I was a valuable team player and could teach him some things. He could offer me new opportunities as well.

Having a good relationship with your boss helps. I really valued the things I learned from people I worked for over the years. Twenty-five years later I'm still learning from my bosses. You can always learn something new, even when you're managing your own department. There is always someone who can offer you new insights and understanding of the work you do no matter how long you do it.

Today I am a vice president and director of marketing at Penguin USA, one of the largest publishing conglomerates in the world. The departments that report to me are advertising, promotion, and publicity. When I look back, I realize my first year in publishing was the most critical one of my life. The training I received during this formative year helped me get the position I have today. These days I no longer produce a one-page flyer for our sales reps to use during sales calls. I'm now responsible for creating complex marketing campaigns that include working with such huge companies as Burger King, TWA, and Hilton International. I have to look for new and fresh ways to increase sales and find new opportunities for sales. During the past Summer Olympics, all the business press discussed the cross-promotional efforts of today's biggest corporations such as Warner Music Group, Coca-Cola, and the Olympics Committee. What emerged from this combined strength was that together these organizations could reach unheard-of numbers of consumers. By themselves, they were impressive enough. Together they were an unbeatable marketing combination. I like to apply the same principles to publishing, which is no less global. The combined clout of a major publishing conglomerate and one of the biggest fast-food chains or airlines is also an unbeatable combination. In addition, I have publicized some great writers such as Stephen King, Erica Jong, Robin Cook, Peter Straub, Ken Follett, Ann Rule, Jonathan Kellerman, and many more. I have created publicity campaigns for categories of books, imprints, newsworthy events, corporate plans, and most recently a Topaz Historical Romance campaign, choosing a gorgeous cover model to be a coverboy and spokesperson for the line. I work with advertising agencies creating ad campaigns for TV, radio, newspapers, and magazines. And the point-of-purchase displays, posters, bookmarks, and the like that you see in bookstores are under my domain. It's a total marketing effort.

For those of you who are about to enter your first year in

publishing, try marketing. Marketing in book publishing is a worthy goal. I'd like to welcome you to the most fascinating, creative, and rewarding career imaginable.

Maryann Palumbo is vice president, director of marketing, mass market at Penguin USA. Mass-market imprints include Signet, Onyx, Signet Classics, Mentor, Topaz, ROC, and DAW Books. She has worked in the publishing field for twenty-five years and loves it today even more than when she originally got hooked.

15

Hey, Lady, Ya Wanna Buy a Book? or My First Year as a Traveling Book Salesman

GREGORY BRANDENBURGH

I emerged from graduate school at the University of Kent at Canterbury in 1978 without any clear career goals. I knew that I did not want to be an academic or an accountant and doubted that I had the talent for either brain surgery or rocket science. I felt that I ought to be engaged in some sort of professional activity that contributed to "the greater good."

By the fall of 1979, I decided that I would either enter the Peace Corps and give my life to a humanitarian cause or find an editorial position with a publishing house and devote my life to the intellectual betterment of society. I completed the Peace Corps applications and sent seventy-five résumés to publishing houses in the United States and in England. Six months later, I began to feel a sense of desperation. I had only two interviews with publishers, neither of which resulted in a job offer, and the Peace Corps bureaucracy was moving at the speed of the peace process in the Middle East. I began to have nightmares of a future as the "funny" son who spent his life caring for his elderly parents.

By June of 1980, I was employed. It was not the job I had wanted or expected. But it was a job—and it was a job in publishing. I became one of two sales representatives based in California for a small evangelical Christian publishing house called Fleming H. Revell.

My territory stretched from Fresno, California, north to the Canadian border and east to the Nebraska state line. I was given $5,000, told to buy a reliable new car, and sent out on the road for training with a senior sales representative.

So began my first year in the glamorous world of publishing. It was to be a year that changed my life: not only a year that established me in the profession but also a year in which I learned all kinds of lessons that contributed to my growth as a human being. The following are the ten most important.

LESSON 1

Publishing is a business, and business isn't always nice.

I began my publishing career with naive notions of what would be entailed in selling books to religious bookstores. I imagined that my first sales call would begin with an enthusiastic greeting from the bookstore owner. We would proceed to the back of the tastefully decorated shop for an uninterrupted hour-long discussion of great literature. The bookstore owner would then order ten copies of every new book, give me profuse thanks for taking the time to visit him, and I would depart feeling intellectually and emotionally stimulated and gratified.

My first sales call shattered those illusions. I arrived with my boss at a religious bookstore located at what could be described euphemistically as an urban area in transition. A Bible verse was spray-painted on the side of the store. The owner explained that he had discovered that street gangs would not further deface his building if it bore a religious message.

The interior of the store was vintage Great Depression. Dusty books were stacked haphazardly everywhere. The majority of the space was devoted to religious merchandise (e.g., plaques with messages such as, "No matter what you do, His blood's for you," and "He's the Real Thing," religious T-shirts and bumper stickers, religious tapes and records, and ceramic figurines of children with very large eyes).

We arrived at eleven in the morning. The manager was cordial in a distant sort of way. We were waved to the front of the store and told to check his inventory. The next hour and a half was spent sorting through stacks of books, checking to see which of my employer's titles were in stock. This was followed by an expensive lunch with the store owner and his wife, which in turn was followed by a twenty-minute sales presentation.

It became clear that the bookstore owner was not particularly well-read and was not interested in discussing the great intellectual issues of our time. He was interested in only three things:

1. Will this book sell?
2. Why will my customers want this book?
3. What will be my discount from the publisher?

The entire experience was disheartening. I was convinced my choice of career was a horrible mistake. I should have joined the Peace Corps and moved to a miserably poor third-world country.

With the benefit of hindsight, I now realize that it was extremely beneficial to confront reality that first day of my new career. There would be sales calls at attractive, well-run bookstores, staffed by intelligent, cultured, and amusing retailers. However, the reality was, and is, that publishing is a business; a business that often involves dealing with less than ideal people and circumstances. The challenge was, and always will be, learning to deal with people in less than ideal situations.

LESSON 2

Every customer is an individual.

In order to be effective, discover what motivates your customer and tailor your presentations accordingly. If the bookseller operates out of a sense of mission, emphasize how a particular book will help his or her customers. This is an especially useful approach in the religious book trade, where many booksellers are in business to do good, not just to earn a living. If the bookseller is primarily interested in profits, present books in terms of their sales potential. If the bookseller has a strong competitive streak, tell her how many copies of a particular book were sold by the bookstore down the street.

LESSON 3

Let the booksellers tell you about their market.

They are dealing with the public on a daily basis. You aren't. Assume that they know more than you do about the clientele they are trying to reach. Find out what is and is not selling. Take that information and work it into your sales presentations.

LESSON 4

Keep sales presentations simple, lively, and concrete.

My first sales presentation went something like this: "This is a book about the age-old problem of suffering presented in the contexts of psychology, theology, and philosophy. The author is a noted ethicist. He explores the various ways in which people have dealt with the intellectual and spiritual issue of suffering and . . ."

After two or three sales calls, my boss drew me aside and suggested that I try a more direct and concrete approach. The second approach went something like this: "What do you do when you lose your job, your wife gets cancer, your daughter runs off with your minister, and your house burns down? We all face tough times, and this is a book that shows people how to cope with life's disasters. The author has written best-selling books for ————— and speaks to large groups around the country on a regular basis."

The second approach worked.

LESSON 5

Learn to think on your feet.

I once had a customer say that she felt the Lord was telling her to order three copies of a new book. I responded with, "That's funny, I think the Lord wants you to buy ten copies." We compromised. She bought six copies.

LESSON 6

Keep your cool.

I met with a buyer in a metaphysical bookstore who could not decide how many copies to purchase of a major new book. She finally asked to lay her hands on the catalog so that she could "feel the vibrations." I wanted to respond with a snort of disbelief or a withering comment. I wisely kept my mouth shut. The vibrations were positive. She ordered a significant quantity.

LESSON 7

Maintain your sense of humor.

Humor keeps the customer's attention, keeps you interested in the task at hand, and gives the presentation an edge.

Often in the middle of a presentation of a somber or pious book to a Christian bookstore manager, I would suddenly thrust into his hands the cover of *The Doctor's Guide to You and Your Colon.* It never failed to amuse me. It also helped to create a sense that the unpredictable could happen during the sales call. People tend to pay close attention when they believe that anything can happen.

LESSON 8

Know your books. Know the markets.

In selling religious books, I found it crucial to understand the differences between Roman Catholic, evangelical Christian, New Age, and mainline Protestant books and to have a clear understanding of which books were appropriate for each store.

For example, I once made the mistake of trying to sell a cookbook that had a bottle of wine on the cover to a conservative Christian bookseller. I had not noticed the wine bottle. It was a minor element of the cover. However, the bookseller was livid. He assumed that I was not taking into account the idiosyncrasies of his market, that I was not paying attention to his needs.

The flip side of steering a bookseller away from a book inappropriate for a particular market is steering him or her toward books that are not religious in content but which appeal to religious people. General health books, certain children's books, and reference books could all be placed in many religious accounts. Occasionally, universal human concerns transcend the barriers of sectarianism.

LESSON 9

Learn when to keep your mouth shut.

Religious booksellers often made statements with which I strongly disagreed. These statements ran the gamut from assertions that a cabal of 24,000 secular humanists had infiltrated and was controlling all business, government, and church organizations in the United States to peculiar conspiracy theories about the religious right.

I learned the hard way that the fastest way to harm a business relationship with a zealot is to express a contrary religious or political opinion. Zealots don't care what you think. You are not going to change their minds. Keep your mouth shut, and save the sale.

LESSON 10

Don't lose your temper when you are treated badly.

This is a difficult concept for everyone, especially me. I generally favor a direct and forceful response to bad behavior. However, maintaining a lucrative business relationship often dictates a gracious response to nasty people.

In difficult situations, I try to process my anger by telling myself: "This person is a jerk. He should pay for his misbehavior. I will make him pay by showing him I am a class act. I will be so gracious, so cooperative, so kind, that he will agonize over his own bad behavior." There is a certain amount of pleasure to be derived from causing an unpleasant person psychic discomfort.

My most vivid recollection of this kind of situation occurred quite early in my first year of selling. I introduced myself to the owner of a religious bookstore in California. He responded by publicly berating me and throwing me out of his store. It is rather disconcerting to be screamed at when you introduce yourself. I swore that never again would I have anything to do with that man.

My boss saw the situation differently. He agreed that the bookstore owner had acted inappropriately; however, he insisted that the situation could be salvaged. He asked that I fill up the trunk of my car with books recently ordered by the angry retailer and that I deliver them to the store.

The result: The bookstore owner felt guilty for verbally assaulting me. He appreciated my rushing his books directly from our warehouse. From that day forward, he always treated me cordially and with respect. But, more important, the business relationship was secure.

My first year in publishing was a long year. It involved driving over 50,000 miles, becoming familiar with airports, hotels, and freeways in every urban area in western America, and being away from home for as much as a month at a time. It was a year in which I learned about myself. I learned that I could sell and that selling was fun. I learned how to get along with difficult people, learned to think on my feet, and learned a modicum of discretion.

In short, that year on the road was a short course in socialization for Greg Brandenburgh.

In the wee hours of the morning after a particularly trying day, I have often wondered what my life would have been if the Peace Corps had responded with greater alacrity to my application. Of course, that question is unanswerable. Greg Brandenburgh in the Peace Corps would have had an entirely different set of experiences and most likely an entirely different kind of life. Not necessarily better or worse. Just different.

What I do know is that today I thoroughly enjoy what I do. I have a career in which I interact with people around the world on a daily basis. I am surrounded by intelligent, creative, and aggressive people who love their jobs. Most important, I am in an environment in which work is more than work—it is also fun. And if work isn't fun, what's the point?

Gregory Brandenburgh is vice president, international publishing at HarperCollins San Francisco. He is a graduate of Gordon College in Wenham, Massachusetts, and the University of Kent in Canterbury, England. He has been with HarperCollins since 1981. He currently spends his days talking on the phone to people in London, Sydney, Auckland, Toronto, New York, and Tokyo. He believes that each workday brings a new high and yet another opportunity of "bending people to his will."

16

Champagne Corks and Mafia Killers

 WILLIAM PARKHURST

When I was a kid in Manchester, New Hampshire, any movie that rolled its opening credits over the skyline of Manhattan got my attention. My fantasy had a soundtrack—motion riffs over honking cabs, murmuring pedestrians—"Hey, buster, why dont-cha watch where you're goin'!"—men in business suits and felt hats, determinedly heading into elevators to do something *important*. (Women were secretaries and/or love interests.)

Two of my favorite New York-at-work films were about book publishing, *Return to Peyton Place* and *The Best of Everything*, but those two films seemed to convey caveats as well as the excitement of the city.

In *Return to Peyton Place*, Jeff Chandler puffed a pipe as he explained Manhattan to Carol Lynley, the virgin novelist just off the bus from New Hampshire herself. "New York," said Jeff, as he took in some smoke, "is like falling in love with the wrong woman." He was her editor, so he had to be both wise and a pipe smoker. "You know she's bad for you, but you just can't stay away." Next came a meaningful gaze, and you just knew the man had big-time pain in his background—wrong-woman pain—and Carol was going to make it better. "As my idol, Max Perkins, once said . . ."

Of course, the poor waif had never heard of Maxwell Perkins or, from the look on her face, any of his authors, but the prematurely gray Chandler told her with an amused wince that in her hometown of Jackass Crossing, New Hampshire, and every other backwater hamlet in America, there was surely a library with a battered copy of Thomas Wolfe's *You Can't Go Home Again*, a monument to the birthing of genius that is the legacy of Perkins and the mission of all real editors.

In *The Best of Everything*, Hope Lange, fresh from Vassar, began her publishing career as she stepped softly into the office of her new boss, an aging, embittered Joan Crawford. Crawford was the "career woman," whose supreme nastiness sounded a warning not to squander childbearing years on work.

In the winter of 1974, I was finding New York a little less fun than those movies. I was working at a radio talk show booking guests, and I was looking for something else. I'd been a disc jockey and news reporter in New England from age eighteen on; I'd served in the navy aboard a destroyer and graduated from the University of New Hampshire. I'd been married and divorced and had financial obligations. Public relations interested me, but so did almost anything that paid more than I was making.

At the radio show, we were always on the phone with book publicists. I figured I'd one day be a writer myself and that working with authors would be fun as well as educational. I'd heard Pocket Books, the paperback division of Simon & Schuster, had an opening in the publicity department. I spoke with Barbara Hendra, the publicity director, but, after four weeks, I decided that she wasn't interested.

As winter turned to spring, then late spring, I decided I didn't want to work at all. I'd always been too responsible. At twenty-eight, I had one final ember of youth. I would do something goofy and freewheeling. I paid my bills a couple of months ahead and was about to find out which old friends were single and in need of a roommate. I'd live on the beach or something. Maybe this would be the hippie era I'd missed because I joined the navy and got married way too young. No more Mr. Responsible. Now I'd be Mr. Hang Loose and, damn it, blow off the summer. Then Ms. Hendra called and invited me in for an interview.

Mass-market paperback publishing was invented at Pocket Books, and the offices, across from St. Patrick's Cathedral at Rockefeller Center, bore the import of that history. Fresh books, like fresh bread, put out an intoxicating aroma that is the signature smell of publishing. I didn't think I'd get the job or take it if it was offered, but I loved that smell and felt instantly at home.

Ms. Hendra's large corner office overlooked the skating rink and even had a view of the Empire State Building. Though single and a career woman, she bore no resemblance to Joan Crawford's bitter character. Ms. Hendra was very much in charge and obviously glad to be where she was. She'd come into the field in the early 1960s at Fawcett and was about to become a vice president of Simon & Schuster.

"Why do you want to work in publishing?" she asked.

I threw out a few platitudes about how I'd taken a lot of calls from publicists and felt I would be able to book authors on talk shows myself. It sounded remote to me; I really wanted to be on the beach, barefoot in the sand. But that delicious smell of new books brought me sharply back to Ms. Hendra's questions. I began to get interested and paid close attention to her next question.

"Tell me how you would book an author in Boston, since you know the media there."

Apparently, I answered right because Barbara Hendra then did something that I have marveled at for nearly two decades. She hired me, despite my having no publishing or publicity experience, to be the senior publicist at Pocket Books.

On June 10, 1974, I started my career in publishing in an office next to Barbara's. I smoked a pipe in those days, and I had to believe it was only a matter of time before I told some babe that New York was like being in love with the wrong woman. But before I could do that, I had a problem. I didn't know anything about the work I'd just been hired to do. Zip. I knew nothing about the acquisition, marketing, or production of books. I knew nothing about working with authors, and, confidence notwithstanding, I didn't know the logistics of setting up a media tour.

I was billed as a radio and television person with extensive media experience that would translate into book publicity in due time. Meanwhile, my coworkers were supposed to accept me as senior. This, I'm sure, went over really big with the rest of the department, all women, all experienced publicists, all making less than my starting salary of $11,500 per year. (It had been explained to me, as it is to young college graduates today, that book publishing is a noble calling that does not pay well.)

And there weren't many men. Len Foreman, the director of advertising and promotion, was Barbara's boss.

"How do you feel about working for a woman?" he asked me during a brief interview.

"Fine, I think, sir. I guess it depends on which woman."

"Well, this woman will teach you a lot because she's the best. But she's also very tough."

Barbara's philosophy of on-the-job training was, basically, figure it out, that's why I hired you. She did have a word of warning before I set up a meeting with my first author, Nancy Friday.

"You can't be tentative with her," she said. "Act like you know what you're doing."

"But I—uh. Can I wait a few days before I meet her?"

"No. The book's out there already."

"What am I supposed to be talking to her about?"

"Oh, five cities. Boston, New York, Philadelphia, Washington, Chicago to start."

"Right."

A five-city tour. Across the hall from me, a young publicist named Cherie Stawascz was working on twenty-five cities for a man who had written a book about bicycles. Five cities with a best-seller seemed reasonable.

I opened Nancy's book, *My Secret Garden: Women's Sexual Fantasies,* figuring, quite wrongly, that you have to know a book well enough to take a test on it before you meet its author. I'd studied it the weekend before, but I wanted one more run-through. *My Secret Garden* had become a best-seller in hardcover thanks to the usual wave a successful book must catch—editorial content that is fresh and captures the imagination of the public, Nancy's interview stamina, and excellent publicity, in this case by my predecessor in the department, Jo-Ann Rhody. I thumbed through Jo-Ann's old publicity schedules, print interviews, publicity reference manuals, and the book itself. What would I say to this author?

I dialed the number.

"Hello."

"Ah, Miss, Ms. Friday?"

"Yes?"

"Uh, this is Bill Parkhurst. I just joined the publicity department of Pocket Books, uh . . ."

Don't be tentative. Act as if you know what you're doing.

"Where did you work before?" she asked, very coolly, no carnal interest whatsoever in her voice.

In radio you are taught to combine volume with downward inflection on your syllables to convey authority when you're reading news.

" 'The Barry Farber Show,' WOR. Barry, by the way, says hi, and he'd *love* to have you back." True on both counts. I hadn't booked the segment, but the segment producer told me she was great.

"Well, isn't that nice. Of course I'll do it."

But I wasn't out of danger.

"So you've done this before, Bill?"

Downward inflection.

"Well, not *here*, of course, but in ten years of broadcasting, you get to know the media landscape pretty well."

"What did you have in mind for my paperback?"

My eyes darted around the room for inspiration. Publicity information comes from computerized manuals that list the nation's local and national talk shows, print media, and newspeople. I grabbed one and flipped it open to a yellow tab marked "Washington."

"For your tour, I thought we'd start in—Washington."

"With what show?"

I ran my finger across the looseleaf page. " 'Take It from Here' at WRC-TV."

"Who are you talking to there?"

I was saved by the producer's italicized name.

"Sheila Weidenfeld."

"Oh, Sheila. Nice person. What about Philadelphia?"

Another yellow tab, another flip.

"Let's target the 'Marciarose Show,' " I said. "KYW-TV."

"Great. She is a *lady*, that Marciarose."

"Sure is."

Before I met with Nancy Friday in Barbara Hendra's office that afternoon, I memorized the key shows and the names of their producers in the cities Nancy would visit. Barbara helped by selling the author on my years of broadcasting experience and recent toil in the arena of talk shows. "Bill knows media from the *inside*," she said.

"I'm sure we're going to get along fine," said Nancy.

I learned way too soon that a senior publicist is expected to handle the promotion of seven or eight titles at one time, write press releases, and fill in on the projects of others in the department during colleagues' absences or vacations.

My second day at Pocket Books brought my next author, Gerard I. Nierenberg, author of *Meta-talk*, a how-to book about interpreting the hidden meaning in conversation. Nierenberg, a lawyer who had written a best-seller on negotiating, never tired of publicity or persuading people to do it for him. By the time I got him, *Meta-talk* had already been out six months, and Jerry had done piles of interviews including "The Tonight Show."

"Johnny loved the interview," he told me. "Loved it. Wants to do it again. Can you set it up?"

Nierenberg, by all accounts, had been a good guest on "The Tonight Show," but the producer didn't want him back. "Interesting segment, but we're not about to do it again," the producer told me.

Nierenberg was unfazed. "They'll redo it. Call them back in a few days. They'll book it again." And, every few days, I'd hear from Jerry asking how my conversation with "The Tonight Show" went. Jerry Nierenberg taught me a basic truth during one of our phone calls.

"Do you want to be president of Simon & Schuster?"

I did not, but he wouldn't have understood anyone who didn't want to run the company some day.

"Yes, I do, Jerry. Any suggestions?"

"You *will* be president of Simon & Schuster if you can figure out one thing."

"Which is?"

Pause.

"You want to be president of Simon & Schuster?"

"Listen, Jerry, I kind of have to get back on the phone—"

"Find a way to get books in the stores when authors tour. Do that one thing, and you will be president of Simon & Schuster. Or any other publishing company you choose."

Yeah right, I thought. Authors never see their books enough, or appropriately displayed. We send memos to the sales department when we book a tour, and the sales staff see that the books are stocked. I was soon to learn that Jerry Nierenberg was absolutely correct. No human being has yet figured out a way to coordinate bookseller inventory with publicity. A possible exception is the case of an author who consistently makes the *New York Times* bestseller list, but even that's just high odds. I would hear even from the most successful authors that books often were not in the stores when they toured.

My first week in publishing ended on a traditional note. People leave publishing houses a lot. You can go to a going-away party any Friday afternoon. You don't have to know the person leaving. Just show up, have some wine, and gossip. My first was my most memorable.

Roxanne, Barbara's secretary, was leaving. Roxanne was very well liked, and someone got the idea to see her off with champagne. We all gathered in Barbara's office to open it.

"Would it be sexist to ask how you are at opening champagne?" Barbara asked me.

"Hell no," I said. "Back in New Hampshire, I'm the one they always call to do it." I was really eager that my new colleagues be impressed. I'd been in my office all week too terrified to stop booking Nancy Friday and Jerry Nierenberg, so they hadn't gotten the chance to view my capabilities, one of them being opening champagne bottles without spilling foam.

But the method that worked in New England didn't play at Rockefeller Center. I forgot I was twenty-seven floors above the heads of swarming tourists. I took the bottle, pointed the neck out an open window, and, before they realized what I was going to do, let the cork fly about thirty feet into the sky. My new colleagues looked on in stunned silence.

"Uh," Barbara said, "in New York we open champagne so the cork doesn't go flying." She looked nervously out the window and listened for the sound of ambulances. When none came, we continued the celebration.

I learned that there are two very broad categories of book publicity. Sometimes the media is so hot for a book that you have to tell them they can't have the author; and sometimes you have to go begging for exposure. You learn to trade off. If someone is nice enough to book the author no one wants, you show up with a celebrity as a reward.

At Pocket Books, we had a good mix of authors, from Donald Barthelme on the literary side to the best-selling author of fiction in the world, Harold Robbins.

Robbins was among that rarefied category of authors who never had to come to the publishing house. His editors and the presidents of both Pocket Books and Simon & Schuster paid their respects to him at the Plaza Hotel, where we kept two suites for him, one for his press interviews and one for his family. If he wanted caviar at midnight, a private jet, two limousines from the airport (one for his family, one for the luggage), Harold Robbins only had to say so.

On one prior tour, his agent had insisted on a Lear Jet and a rock band to greet him at each stop. Fortunately, Robbins decided to travel by airliner and to can the rock band, but if he'd wanted all these things, he'd have gotten them. I was awestruck by the raw power of stardom.

There was a reason for this treatment beyond catering to the ego of the author, considerable as that was. Robbins, a former movie publicity person himself, made his millions not by writing about sex, which was popularly supposed, but by writing about glamour and power and the rise from poverty to wealth. He lived this life and understood that he was selling it every time he did an interview.

The man himself was rather soft-spoken and, in my view, easy to get along with. What impressed me most was his ability to remember names, always a useful skill to have. He ties with Robert Ludlum for the best-selling writer with the best memory for the names of all the people, major and minor, around him. Like Nancy Friday, and unlike a thousand lesser lights, Robbins was a worker. While on tour, he was never too important to speak to anyone.

The producer of a local newscast decided to do a "life-style" piece featuring Robbins and asked me to have plenty of Dom Perignon, Beluga caviar, and beautiful women on hand at the press suite at three o'clock on a Monday. We did, and we were canceled for a bank explosion. The caviar was excellent. The producer called back. Could we reschedule for tomorrow? Again the champagne and the caviar, again the models, and again the crew went elsewhere, but Mark Monsky, news director of Channel 5, swore they'd get this piece done.

Robbins himself drank Fresca and seemed unimpressed with

the Beluga, asking the hotel's crew to hold off opening it until we saw television cameras. I was disappointed. They finally made it, we had our "Life in the Fast Lane" piece, and I got to chomp on more caviar.

Robbins was deeply confident of his place in literary history, far more so than John Irving, Saul Bellow, or any other author I got to meet in this business. "I am better than Hemingway, better than Steinbeck, and certainly better than Joyce," he told interviewers. "The people make literature," he often said, "not reviewers." Uh, okay.

His first sale had been to a very classy publishing house, Alfred A. Knopf, and even his most caustic critics had to admit that his novel *A Stone for Danny Fisher* proved a power not seen in, say, *The Carpetbaggers.*

Whatever his place in the annals of literature, Robbins was not a great interview, and we had some trouble getting him on "The Today Show." This is where Barbara Hendra earned her money exponentially. She could get a dancing gnat on "The Today Show." In the days before "Good Morning America" and other morning talk shows, "The Today Show" was the defining moment of a successful book tour. And Barbara could always deliver it. As part of our job, we were expected to watch all national television appearances of any author being handled by the department, whether or not we were directly involved.

One morning I crawled out of bed to watch Barbara Walters interview a woman named Danielle McCafferty, author of a book called *Celebration,* an original paperback on creative wedding planning. I thought the timing of the book was stupid because it was published in June when it was probably too late to be of much use to a bride.

But I was pretty impressed with the author, and even though she was advising brides, she was divorced, like me. Cherie

Stawascz, who handled Danielle's publicity, noticed my interest and introduced me to her in the office. "Why don't you join us at 'AM New York' tomorrow morning?" Cherie suggested. "Then we can go to breakfast at Café des Artistes."

I agreed, although I was a night person in those days. I often stayed in the office until after nine in the evening doing paperwork and calling the West Coast. Three or four in the morning was easy for me to see; seven or eight in the morning was not. About half the department, including Barbara, kept such hours, so there was no problem with my nocturnal ways.

I had just moved into a studio apartment on the Upper West Side of Manhattan, and when I rolled out of the shower the next morning, I remembered that my underwear was still packed. I grabbed a pair of clean shorty pajamas and put them on under my pants. My father wore boxer shorts all his life. I could live with them for one day.

"AM New York," a distant forerunner to "Regis and Kathy Lee," was nearby, and I trotted over there. A publicist should work the room in a studio, so I made sure I met the producers, the host, the makeup person, the guy who brought donuts to the green room, and the security guard. I also gushed to Danielle about how well she had done on the show.

Across the street at Café des Artistes, we talked about the process of writing *Celebration* and being an author. Danielle was the first person I'd met who was my age and did such a thing. Gosh, what was it like? She was friendly, but the sparks didn't fly. I took it philosophically. The women in the department told each other never to date an author, so I assumed it applied to me as well.

When I got back to Pocket Books, I went into the men's room and about keeled over when I saw myself in the mirror. When I got dressed at dawn, I had tucked my shirt in the waist of my pajamas, and the elastic band was a full three inches above my belt. I'd been walking around that way all morning.

I let out a howl of anguish.

I could hear noise coming out of my mouth, but I could not stop it. Curses! I doubled over, pounded the sink, looked again, and cursed again. That's when Len Foreman, my boss's boss, came out of one of the stalls.

"Uh, I, uh, did a stupid thing," I said, trying to explain.

"That's quite all right, Bill," Len said. "I don't think I want to hear any more about it."

About three weeks into my career, Barbara came into my office. "I need you to find Joey," she said. "They want to interview him in Dallas. I'd love for you to handle him."

I gulped. Joey was one of our authors and also an alleged Mafia killer. He found out that someone in the company had been having an affair with a married author, then threatened to tell the man's wife if she didn't meet him for a weekend in Detroit. He could, and did, intimidate.

Joey was reached by a series of calls to intermediaries. He always called back collect. Our first conversation was interrupted by the Simon & Schuster operator, whose instructions were to never accept a collect call.

"Collect call to Mr. Parkhurst from—who are you again?"

"Joey."

"May I have your number so Mr. Parkhurst can call you back on the WATS line?"

"Just tell him it's Joey. He'll take the call."

"One moment, Joy. We're trying to get him."

"Not Joy, hon, Joey."

"Mr. Joey who?"

"Just Joey."

"May I have your last name please?"

"Joey, *Joey, Joey,* and tell Parkhurst I'm going to kick his goddam ass if he doesn't get on the line and take the call."

"I'm here, operator. That will be fine."

Joey wrote three books for us, *Killer, Hit #29,* and *Joey Kills.* I would publicize all of them, and he would never intimidate me. He would also never give up on the notion that I was supposed to find him a date.

It is a bizarre testament to some darkness in the human soul that this killer—and several investigative reporters told me he really was a hit man—found no shortage of women who were turned on by him. He was short, barrel-chested, and kind of oily, but I got used to a certain sympathy toward Joey from some women admirers who booked him on their shows.

"Oh, it's the way he was brought up. It's the code by which he lives," one frequent female companion told me. "He's really a nice guy."

He really was a nice guy. I had many meals with him, put him on the phone with my daughter when she was four, and constantly heard about how much it bothered him when his dog died. He was a nice killer.

"Blowing people away is my business," he said. "It's not personal."

"Except to the person you're blowing away, I assume," I told him. "But you wouldn't kill me if, say, something went a little wrong with your interviews, Joe?"

"Nah. You're a buddy. Besides, I don't kill no one for under twenty grand, and no one's going to pay me twenty grand to do you."

Thus reassured, I kept booking him.

Television loved Joey. He would slip into the studio, put on a Halloween mask or an executioner's hood, and do a riveting interview. We got most of the taped national shows—"Tom Snyder,"

"David Susskind," "Mike Douglas"—but certain programs such as "Donahue," then in its first year in Chicago, couldn't book him as a guest because Joey would not go on live television. He claimed the mob would kill him. Eventually, they did just that.

Penny Price of "The Mike Douglas Show" called me one day asking if we knew of a good psychiatrist, who might go on with Joey. We had one touring, Dr. David Viscott, author of *How to Live with Another Person.*

"No shrinks," Joey said.

"I know, Joey," I told him, "but it would really help us out if you would do it. We can promote two of our books at once."

"Is he, like a pretty good guy?"

"Oh, yeah. No problem."

"He's not going to ask me all that shrink stuff?"

"Well, a little, but David's a good guy."

Actually, Dr. Viscott was handled by Lesleigh Lad, another publicist in the department. I didn't know him at all.

"All right, I'll do it."

Dr. Viscott's first question to Joey was how it felt to kill someone.

"What are you, a yo-yo?" Joey asked.

It got worse. Joey threatened to blow poor Dr. Viscott away. Someone from "The Mike Douglas Show" called me afterward. It was, she said, Great Television.

The radio and television booking of my first year was only the operational edge of the new career, the front door to a great industry. I didn't know it at the time, but I got into publishing just in time to see the yesterdays of Simon & Schuster.

Nineteen seventy-four was the final year for old-timers at the company. You could still talk to Leon Shimkin, the "third S" who was the financial soul of Simon & Schuster and, effectively, the owner of the joint. Len Foreman had been there over twenty-five years, and the warrens and cubicles of our two floors at One West Thirty-ninth Street, where most of the employees worked, were full of people in their fifties and sixties who had been doing their jobs on one basic assumption—devote yourself to a company, and it will take care of you.

A year later, Leon sold us to Gulf & Western, the megaconglomerate that included Paramount Pictures. We were in the movie business and the cattle business; we owned the New York Knicks and Madison Square Garden. Mostly, we were in the youth business. Dick Snyder, at age forty, became the new president and CEO of Simon & Schuster. Soon many key people were in their thirties. I thought I survived the era because I was good. I now think I made it because I was young and inexpensive.

Len Foreman was made director of special projects, moved to an office out of the way, his secretary placed in the hall. As in most corporations, director of special projects means you're either on the way in, ready to pounce on someone's job, or on the way out. Len, after more than a quarter of a century, disappeared one lunch hour and left me a good-bye note.

Leon Shimkin was very well paid, but he was ushered out without much dignity. He may have known money, but I doubt if he knew big corporation psychology. Officially a consultant, he probably thought they'd consult him.

"I hope he doesn't make me kick his ass," said one of the senior Gulf & Western people in Barbara's office one night. "Let him be, you know—"

"The elder statesman, the greak link to the past?" I chimed in.

"Yeah, right. The elder statesman. But if he gets in my way, I'm going to kick his ass. I have no choice." By training, the butt kicker was an accountant.

The faces in the warrens and cubicles became young, fresh, and enthusiastic. The departing old-timers said that publishing had lost its soul. It would now be run by M.B.A.'s with no sense of books. The whole editorial wing of Pocket Books got sent home in a single morning. I saw this happen twice in my two and a half years at Simon & Schuster. I don't know that publishing has lost its soul. The changes more likely reflect postmodern reading habits, and, to me, it's a miracle that anyone reads books at all.

In 1977, Barbara and I made news when we left Pocket Books together to run various publicity departments for the Putnam Publishing Group. Letty Pogrebin interviewed us for an article in the *Ladies Home Journal,* which asked, "Can a Man Work for a Woman?" There are more men in publicity now. At the luncheons of the Publishers Publicity Association, the field's trade group, you see rows of young men as well as women.

Barbara Hendra set up her own public relations firm in 1979 and still produces megapublicity. I stayed in the field for seven years and, in 1981, also set up my own company, a media consulting firm. We train authors for radio and television and produce syndicated radio features for publishers.

Most of the major publishers, including Pocket Books, are my clients. The company, like most of the former paperback houses, is now very much a hardcover publisher as well. My most recent project for Pocket Books was to produce a radio interview syndication with Nancy Friday for *Women on Top,* her sequel to *My Secret Garden.*

"We've really come full circle, haven't we?" Nancy said on the phone when we talked recently.

"We really have."

Then her voice took on a well-remembered tone. "Tell me again what you have in mind."

I explained the process of radio syndication with downward inflection, still acting, after nineteen years, as if I know what I am doing.

William Parkhurst, president of Parkhurst Communications, is a former publicity director of the Berkley Publishing Corporation, Richard Marek Publishers, Perigee, and Avon Books. For seven years he served as host of "NightTalk," an author interview program on New York's WOR radio. He is the author of How to Get Publicity, The Eloquent Executive, *and* True Detectives *and has been on tour three times.*

17

Ignorance and Curiosity

R O B E R T B . W Y A T T

My first year in publishing lasted two years, and in that period I learned everything that would serve me in publishing "proper" for the next three decades. I sold books in a New York City bookstore. And I didn't sell just books. I sold paperbacks.

A Greyhound bus brought me to New York on Labor Day, 1962, but it wasn't a bus that drove me to the city. It was that subtle combination of ignorance and curiosity that always has served me well. I didn't realize that the new life I sought probably wasn't in the cards for a guy from Miami, Oklahoma, and just out of the University of Tulsa.

In my senior year at TU I had realized that I did not want to continue working nights at the *Tulsa Daily World.* As a former copyboy turned junior reporter, I knew I couldn't make a living with death and bad weather. My only claims to fame were the bylines on my obituaries of famous Tulsans and my front-page coverage of tornadoes. When I declined the offer of the police beat, I knew my newspaper days would end. I was too squeamish for such work.

I decided then to move to New York at the end of summer and get a job in advertising or book publishing. I had my own odd qualifications. I was probably the only high school student in Ottawa County—perhaps in the state of Oklahoma—who subscribed to *Advertising Age* and decorated his bedroom walls with favorite advertisements ripped from his secondhand issues of the *New York Times*. And I no doubt was the only Miami, Oklahoma, teenager to cover the remaining wall space with the beginning of a personal library of paperback books.

Armed with my fragile credentials, I decided to try book publishing first and fired off dozens of letters to book publishers listed in *Literary Market Place*. I also wrote to John Tebbel, the noted publishing historian, who was running the New York University Graduate Institute of Book Publishing. A few publishers responded courteously, but they could not help the way John Tebbel did. He wrote me that the institute had lost its funding and would not continue. If I wanted, however, to take the chance, he would find *some kind of job* for me in New York City.

Three days from Oklahoma, I arrived at the Port Authority Bus Terminal. My first year in publishing was about to begin. I was armed with only my suitcase and my bus reading—a Pyramid paperback on etiquette and the Scribner Library edition of *Axel's Castle*. The first was essential because I was uncertain about proper big-city behavior. The Edmund Wilson was just for fun.

I moved into the Hotel Broadway Central, which a few years later would literally collapse under the weight of its structural faults, leaving only its notorious history as a haven for stylish reprobates in the early part of the century.

The search for work began.

John sent me to various cronies with whom he had dealt in his distinguished career as editor and scholar. They didn't want me. Hell, I wouldn't have wanted me either.

In time, Doubleday Book Shops hired me as a clerk for its flagship store at 724 Fifth Avenue. The timing was crucial. I was running out of borrowed money, I couldn't afford the Hotel Broadway Central, and I had just rented my first apartment on 106th Street and Riverside Drive. The coffin-shaped room contained only a toilet, kitchen, and bed area, but it fit my financial formula of one week's salary for one month's rent. The ninety bucks from Doubleday met the requirement.

After about ten minutes of employment-processing procedures in the basement offices of the bookshop, I was let loose on the sales floor. I learned how to use the cash register, how to clean books, and how to address fellow employees as Mr. or Mrs. or Miss. I would be required to wear my suit every day. I figured I could alternate my two ties. I even learned how to disguise my Oklahoma twang with something that sounded about as mid-Atlantic as Greenland.

The boss first assigned me to the front area of the store, which sold current and backlist hardcovers. Upstairs was the remainder section, and toward the back were the juvenile and paperback sections. My time up front was short-lived. The boss discovered I had a propensity for telling customers about the availability of certain hardcover titles in paperback. I did know my paperbacks. Had I not the finest private paperback library in Miami? Had I not reviewed paperbacks for my *Tulsa Collegian* column, "Arts Not So Fine"? Was I not wholly without paperback prejudice, unlike the snotty Scribners' shop down Fifth Avenue, which did not deign to stock mass-market paperbacks? I knew where I belonged, and so did the boss.

And in the move to the paperback department, I got a new boss, a Munchkin, a real live Munchkin, who knew Judy Garland.

Children and short adults were employed in the roles of Munchkins in *The Wizard of Oz*, according to my new boss, who sometimes proved to be an unreliable narrator. He claimed he had worked as a Munchkin on the movie set, where his father was a photographer. Occasionally, his friendship with show business customers verified his Hollywood experiences.

Working for a Munchkin came to have its advantages because he frequently did not show up for work and I could run the department my way. My frustration came upon his return from his hiatuses. It was difficult to relinquish the show I'd been running. He would take off for several weeks at a time and return transformed. He might come back grossly overweight from one absence and then a few months later return as skinny as the Scarecrow. (He also discussed his frequent sexual crises with the staff. I found these very interesting because we didn't have anything like them in Oklahoma.)

He usually managed to keep his hand in from afar. The home office nearby on Madison Avenue had no notion of the kinds of books we sold to our precious carriage trade. The office staff placed the initial orders for each publisher's releases. They knew how to order the James Bonds, but they couldn't understand our needs for more than three copies of the latest Iris Murdoch from Viking Compass or Herman Hesse from New Directions. We could sell fifty copies a week of *A Severed Head* and even more of *Siddhartha*. So as soon as we got copies of the home office orders, we rang up our rep and rewrote the order to fit our store's needs.

Understandably the former Munchkin would not allow me to place the orders by myself, but as his absences became more frequent, I needed instruction. This occurred at his retreat, a chic loony bin on Manhattan's East Side, where I patiently took orders from the madman in the fancy pajamas.

He never returned from one of his absences. The show was mine.

And it was such fun! The best time was Christmas when the first thought of the day was the moment you rang up your first sale and the second thought was the last ring of the day. During the day you went on automatic pilot as you rang up stack after stack of the holiday purchases of the wonderfully wealthy customers.

The only dark moment of the holiday delirium occurred the Christmas of 1963 when the powers of Doubleday and Company decided it would be good for their editorial operation if the company's editors got firsthand experience in bookselling. Wrong. If the editors had been taught to make change, it would have been a different story, but it soon became apparent that there was a cruel disparity between the registers' records and the cash on hand. Our new clerks couldn't figure out how to gift wrap or how to deal with credit cards. Their new role as clerks did not deter them from the standard three-martini publishing luncheon as befit their race, so afternoons were often a bit *odd*. It was the loose change, though, that got them in the end and forever banished them from our operation.

At the time it never occurred to me that I might join that race of editors. I was glad to have a job and a chance to go to museums and catch up on classic films and see famous people. Back in Oklahoma I had never imagined so much could happen to me in New York. Every day was an adventure.

The best New York adventures, though, were always in the shop. It was fun to see how a paperback publisher would dress up a best-seller for its paperback publication, to see if it could bail out a turkey like *Wanderers Eastward, Wanderers West.* New American Library couldn't. Or bail out a dog like *Boys and Girls Together.* Bantam could. Or see how a movie life of T. E. Lawrence could sell loads of different titles about Lawrence of Arabia. Or have a Dell salesman give you your very own copy of the Delta edition of *Cat's Cradle* because all the people at Dell thought that Kurt Vonnegut was really going to break out. Vonnegut's literary career had bounced from hardcovers at Scribners to paperback originals at Fawcett's Gold Medal line. When Seymour Lawrence established his imprint at Delacorte, Vonnegut became one of his early authors, and he galvanized the Delacorte staff members from the editors in the office to the sales force in the field. I learned from my rep about the publishing processes that build an author's career.

I also began to realize that other kinds of publishing personages were customers. They were snoops. Some were editors. Some were publicity people. Some were authors. Often when an editor or author became obvious, we'd punish them. When Jacqueline Susann and her husband came in to check out her dog book, we hid it under the counter after they left. They usually bought the clerks copies of the book and signed them. If they had not signed them, we could have returned them to stock for credit and pocketed a much needed five or six bucks, which was the price of a hardcover book at that time.

We had our favorite customers, and we learned at Doubleday that our biggest asset was a faithful clientele. We wanted those people to stop by on their lunch hour every day. We were convinced they were loaded, and we knew we were there to unload them at Fifty-seventh Street and Fifth Avenue. When we learned they would spend their money on books, we were always there for them. We stocked *The Unquiet Grave* by "Palinurus" because we had a woman who bought five or six a week. If someone liked a Wimsey mystery, we had a Nicholas Blake or a Michael Innes for that individual. I learned that if customers showed interest in American literature and criticism, you showed them the newest titles in this area when they came in on their lunch breaks.

If you are truly ignorant and curious, you might try to sell a book as I once did.

A customer named Mr. Mayer came in nearly daily. I did not know what he did for a living, and I did not care as long as he bought the books I suggested.

I had been following privately the fortunes of Avon Books, a somewhat sleazy paperback line, which had been purchased recently by the Hearst Corporation. Hearst seemed to be refurbishing the line in interesting ways. I observed that Avon seemed to be changing itself by doing such wacky things as rounding the corners of its paperbacks and publishing in mass-market format the likes of Susan Sontag and Michael Gold. I was particularly smitten with Avon's release of an original collection of criticism, *On Contemporary Literature*, edited by Richard Kostelanetz.

When Mr. Mayer sauntered in one afternoon to check things out, I could but peddle him the new title. I had no way of knowing he worked at Avon Books as education editor.

He responded, "Mr. Wyatt, I have to tell you that I published that book, but I sure do appreciate your trying to sell it to me."

I doubt my pleasure in meeting a real, breathing editorial presence outweighed the pain of losing a sale.

A short time later Peter Mayer and Avon had a great success in issuing a paperback edition of the depression-era novel *Call It Sleep* by Henry Roth. I suspect that some of the folks at Avon figured there was no room for their education editor *and* them, so several left when he was named editor-in-chief. He needed a staff.

"Mr. Wyatt, do you want to work as an editor?"

I don't recall precisely how I answered, but in ignorance and curiosity something came out "yes," and I did.

Robert B. Wyatt is president of A Wyatt Book, Inc., and publishes about a dozen books a year under the imprint of A Wyatt Book for St. Martin's Press. After his editorial debut at Avon, he worked as editorial director of books for young readers at Delacorte, returned to Avon as editor-in-chief, and most recently served as editor-in-chief, vice president of Ballantine Books.

Bibliography

This section includes autobiographies, biographies, memoirs, and reminiscences of professionals in book publishing.

Berg, A. Scott. *Maxwell Perkins, Editor of Genius.* New York: Dutton, 1978; New York: Pocket Books, 1979.

Bliven, Bruce. *Book Traveler.* New York: Dodd Mead, 1975.

Brooks, Paul. *Two Park Street: A Publishing Memoir.* Boston: Houghton Mifflin, 1986.

Burlingame, Roger. *Of Making Many Books: A Hundred Years of Reading, Writing and Publishing.* New York: Scribner's, 1946.

Canfield, Cass. *Up & Down & Around: A Publisher Recollects the Time of His Life.* New York: Harper's Magazine Press, 1971.

Cerf, Bennett. *At Random: The Reminiscences of Bennett Cerf.* New York: Random House, 1977.

Commins, Dorothy, ed. *What Is an Editor? Saxe Commins at Work.* Chicago: University of Chicago Press, 1978.

Dana, Robert, ed. *Against the Grain: Interviews with Maverick American Publishers*. Iowa City: University of Iowa Press, 1986.

Doran, George. *Chronicles of Barabbas, 1884–1934*. 2d ed. New York: Holt, Rinehart and Winston, 1952.

Doubleday, F. N. *The Memoirs of a Publisher*. New York: Doubleday, 1972.

Gilmer, Walker. *Horace Liveright: Publisher of the Twenties*. New York: David Lewis, 1970.

Haydn, Hiram. *Words and Faces*. New York: Harcourt Brace Jovanovich, 1974.

Laughlin, James. *Essays: Recollections of a Publisher*. Mt. Kisco, N.Y.: Moyer Bell, 1989.

Madison, Charles A. *The Owl Among Colophons: Henry Holt as Publisher and Editor*. New York: Holt, Rinehart and Winston, 1966.

O'Connor, Patrick. *Don't Look Back: A Memoir*. Mt. Kisco, N.Y.: Moyer Bell, 1993.

————. *So Far So Good*. Mt. Kisco, N.Y.: Moyer Bell, 1993.

Putnam, George Palmer. *Wide Margins: A Publisher's Autobiography*. New York: Harcourt, Brace and Company, 1942.

Regnery, Henry. *Memoirs of a Dissident Publisher*. New York: Harcourt Brace Jovanovich, 1979.

Reynolds, Paul R., Jr. *The Middle Man*. New York: Morrow, 1971.

Schwed, Peter. *Turning the Pages: An Insider's Story of Simon & Schuster, 1924–1984*. New York: Macmillan, 1984.

Scribner, Charles, Jr. *In the Company of Writers: A Life in Publishing*. New York: Scribner's, 1990.

————. *In the Web of Ideas: The Education of a Publisher*. New York: Scribner's, 1993.

Targ, William. *Indecent Pleasures*. New York: Macmillan, 1975.

Index

aa's (author's alterations), 50, 80
Academic Press, 77
acquisitions (acquiring) editors, xx–xxiii,
    24–29, 33–34, 39–40, 49, 50–51
agents, xix–xxi, xxiii, 10–15, 18–19
Alfred A. Knopf, xxvi, 66–73
American Indexing Society, 88
apprenticeship, x–xi, xv–xvi, 6–7, 54–55, 77,
    112
aptitude tests, computerized, 45
art books, 83–84
Association of American Publishers (AAP), xvi
authors, xxv, 10–12, 14, 18–19, 33, 49, 50,
    54, 57, 62–63, 80, 88, 150
Avon Books, 144, 151
A Wyatt Book, xxxiii, 152

Ballantine Books, 152
Bantam Books, 59–60
Barthelme, Donald, 135
Beacon Press, xxviii, 99
Berkley Publishing, 144
Best of Everything, The, 127, 128
Blake, Laura J., xix–xxi, 10–15
Blake, Nicholas, 150
bluelines (blues), 51, 58
booksellers, bookstores, xxx, xxxiii, 21–22,
    93–99, 118–26, 145–52
bound-book dates, 49
Brandenburgh, Gregory, xxi, 118–26
Brooklyn College, 110
Brown, James Oliver, 12
Burning Bed, The (McNulty), 108

California, University of, at Berkeley, 24,
    44–46
Call It Sleep (Roth), 151
career counseling, 8, 35, 36
Carpetbaggers, The (Robbins), 137

Carter, Graydon, 37
Cascardi, Andrea, xxii–xxiii, 30–34
cash flow, 95–96
Cat's Cradle (Vonnegut), 150
catalogs, 113–14
Celebration (McCafferty), 137–38
Cenedella, Betsy, 58
Chamberlain, Narcisse, 59
character flaws, 74–75
Charles Scribner's Sons, xxiii, xxiv, xxv, 31, 43,
    53, 55
chief financial officers (CFOs), xxviii–xxix,
    93–99
children's books, xxii–xxiii, 26, 31–34
Chilton, Lloyd, xxiv, 47–49, 51–52, 53
Christmas sales, 149
City University of New York, 85, 92
"classic" publishing, xi–xii
coffee, making and serving of, x, 46
Cohen, Sydney Wolfe, xxvii–xxviii, 86–92
collections, debt, 94–97
Columbia University, 51, 92
commas, 49, 60–61, 78, 89
compositors, xxvii, 49–50, 70–71, 80, 82–83
computer technology, xv–xvii, xxix–xxx, xxxiii,
    xxxiv
Conyers, Claude, 52
Coptic Encyclopedia, The, 52
copy editors, xxv–xxvi, xxvii, 41, 56–64,
    77–78, 82, 89, 95
copyrights, 12
corporate culture, xxviii, 38, 90–91
covers, xxvi, xxvii, 25–26, 50–51, 72, 79,
    111–12
credit holds, 95
Crown Publishers, xxii, 16–23, 43
Curtis Brown, xix–xx, 11–15
C. W. Post, 92

David R. Godine, Publisher, xxviii, 93–99
Debutante, The (Diliberto), 69
Delacorte, 150, 152
delivering work, 87
demographics, publishing, xxiv, 36, 42–43
Denneny, Michael, 26
Denver, University of, 30–31
designers, xxvi–xxvii, 65–73, 94
design-survey forms, 50
Dictionary of American Biography, 54, 55
Diliberto, Gioia, 69
direct mail, 27
Doremus, Ed, 89–90
Doubleday, xxxiii, 147–51
Dubin, Elyse, xxiv, xxvii, 47–51, 53, 74–85
Dunow, Henry, 11–13
Duras, Marguerite, 38–39

editorial directors, xxi–xxii
editorial production, xxiii, xxv, xxvii, 39, 41,
    49–54, 77–85, 89
editors-in-chief, xxi–xxii, xxiii
education, ix, xvii, xviii, xxii, xxviii, 8–9,
    30–31, 35–37, 44–47, 70, 101–2
employment agencies, 84
Encyclopedia of Religion, 52
Encyclopedia of the Holocaust, 52
encyclopedias, 52–54
English, degrees in, 56, 75–76
entry-level positions, 4–9, 36, 37–38, 48,
    54–55, 78–79, 103, 106
ESL (English as a Second Language) books, 60
executive editors, xxi–xxii, xxxiii, 16–23

Farber, Barry, 132
Farrar, Straus & Giroux, 109
Fawcett, Farrah, 108
Fleming H. Revell, xxxi, 119–26
Foreman, Len, 130, 139, 142
four food groups of publishing, 57, 63
freelancers, 57, 59–61, 71, 73, 77–78, 82, 87,
    91
Friday, Nancy, xxxii, 131–33, 135, 136, 143

Gardner, Erle Stanley, 59
Giangrande, Gregory, xviii–xix, 1–9
Ginsberg, Peter, 11
Godine, David R., 93–94, 96, 98, 99
Gold, Michael, 151
Gordon College, 126

grammar, 49, 56, 78, 82, 89–90
Gulf & Western, 142
Gutenberg, Johannes, xv

hand-selling, xxxiii, 147–51
Harcourt Brace Jovanovich, 103–9
hardcovers, xviii, xxix, xxxii–xxxiii, 38
Harper & Row, 89, 97
HarperCollins Publishers, xxi, 85, 126
Harvard Business School, 94
Havel, Vaclav, 71–72
Healy, Lisa, xv–xxxiv
Hearst Corporation, 151
Hendra, Barbara, 128–31, 134–35, 137, 138,
    139, 143
Herriot, James, 17
Hesse, Herman, 148
Hit #29 (Joey), 140
Holy Cross, 30
Houghton Mifflin, xxii–xxiii, 32–34
house hoppers, 57, 84
housing, 47–48
How to Live with Another Person (Viscott), 141
human resources management, xviii–xix, 1–9
Hyperion Books for Children, xxii, 34
Hyperion/Disney Press, xxix, 109

illustrations, 68, 71, 73, 79, 80, 83–84
indexers, xxvii–xxviii, 50, 57, 59, 86–92
"information superhighway," xxxiii
Innes, Michael, 150
internships, 6–7, 8
interviews, 7–8, 25, 47, 57, 103, 129–30
Intext Press, 112–13

jackets, xxvi, xxvii, 25–26, 50–51, 72, 79,
    111–12
job hunting, 6–8, 16, 31–32, 35–38, 44–48,
    54–55, 76–77, 79, 84, 102–5, 146–47
job turnover, 36, 57, 84, 112
Joey (author), 139–41
Joey Kills (Joey), 140
Johns Hopkins University Press, 26
jokes, 58, 96
journals, 27, 78, 80–81

Kaiserlian, Penny, 26
K&N Bookworks, 64
Kent, University of, at Canterbury, 118, 126
Killer (Joey), 140

Kliemann, Kristin, xxix–xxx, 100–109
Klose, Victoria, xxv–xxvi, 56–64
Knopf, Alfred A., xxxii–xxxiii
Knowlton, Perry, 11
Kostelanetz, Richard, 151

Lad, Lesleigh, 141
Ladies Home Journal, 143
Lawrence, Seymour, 150
Lawrence, T. E., 149–50
Lehman College of the City University of New
    York, 85
Letters to Olga (Havel), 71–72
listening, 27
Literary Market Place, The, xvi, 146
Lover, The (Duras), 38–39
Ludlum, Robert, 136

McCafferty, Danielle, 137–38
McCaig, Donald, 17
Macmillan, xxiv, 47–53, 55, 81
McNulty, Faith, 108
managing editors, xxi, xxiii–xxiv, xxv, xxvii,
    18–21, 39–40, 49, 54, 81–84, 95, 149
manuscripts, reading of, 11, 19, 32
Manutius, Aldus, xii
Margolin, Malcolm, 46
marketing, xxviii, xxix, xxx–xxxii, 27, 110–17
mass-market paperbacks, xviii, xxix, xxx, xxxii,
    145
Mayer, Peter, 151
mechanicals, 71, 80
Medina, Kate, x
mentors, x, xxvii, 6–7, 11–12, 54–55, 77, 79,
    89–90
mergers and acquisitions, 89, 142–43
Meta-talk (Nierenberg), 133
Metropolitan Transit Authority (MTA),
    65–67
Michigan, University of, 56
"midlist" books, xxxii
"Mike Douglas Show, The," 141
Miller, Sylvia K., xxiv–xxv, xxvii, 44–55
Monsky, Mark, 136
Murdoch, Iris, 148
My Secret Garden (Friday), xxxii, 131

names, memory for, 136
networking, 7, 57, 59–61, 88

new books, arrival of, 84–85
New Hampshire, University of, 128
New York, State University of, at Buffalo, 73,
    99
New York Times Book Review, 97–98, 134
New York University, xxi, xxviii, 2, 9, 23,
    44–47, 64, 92, 109, 146
Nierenberg, Gerard I., 133–35
Nop's Trials (McCaig), 17
North Point Press, 44, 98
Novak, Thomas S., xxviii–xxix, 93–99

On Contemporary Literature (Kostelanetz), 151
Open Book Committee (PEN American Cen-
    ter), 42
ornaments, 69, 71, 73
Oxford University Press, 52

Palumbo, Maryann, xxx–xxxi, 110–17
Pantheon/Schocken Books, xxiii–xxiv, 38–41,
    43
paperbacks, xviii, xxix, xxx, xxxii–xxxiii, 25–26,
    145
Paramount Pictures, 142
Parkhurst Communications, xxxi, 144
Parkhurst, William, xxxi–xxxii, 127–44
Peace Corps, 118–19, 126
peanut butter, 48
Penguin, 23, 115–17
Pergamon Press, 78–81
Perigee, 144
pe's (printer's errors), 50
Philipson, Morris, xxii, 24–29
Plato, 1, 9
Pocket Books, xxxii, 128–43
Pogrebin, Letty, 143
Pratt Institute, 65, 73, 75
Price, Penny, 141
printers, 51, 82–84, 114
production (manufacturing) department,
    50–51
production editors, xxiii, xxv, xxvii, 39, 41,
    78–79, 81, 89
professional books, 51
profitability, 20–23, 38, 60, 84
proofreaders, 57–59, 95
Proulx, E. Annie, 48
publicists, xxi, xxxi–xxxii, 127–44
publishers, xxi–xxii
Publishers Publicity Association, 143

publishing courses, ix, xvii, xviii, xxii, xxviii,
    8–9, 30–31, 36–37, 44–47, 70
publishing process, xviii–xxxiii, 25–26, 32, 40,
    49–51
Putnam Publishing Group, 86, 143

quality control, 80, 82

Radcliffe College, 36–37
Random House, x, xix, xxiii, 3, 9, 59, 66
receptionists, 46
Regents Publishing, 60
reproduction proofs (repros), 68
résumés, criteria for, 7, 103
Return to Peyton Place, 127–28
Rhody, Jo-Ann, 131
Rice University, 101
Richard Marek Publishers, 144
Robbins, Harold, 135–37
Roth, Henry, 151
Routledge, 26–27
royalties, 22
Rutgers University, 92

St. Martin's Press, xxxiii, 26, 152
salaries, 4–5, 36, 38, 48, 79, 84, 103, 130
sales and commission representatives, xxx–xxxi,
    97, 118–26
Schiffrin, Andre, xxiv, xxxiii, 38, 41
secretaries, 24–29, 46
Severed Head, A (Murdoch), 148
Shacochis, Bob, 43
Shimkin, Leon, 141–42
Siddhartha (Hesse), 148
Simon, Dolores, 89
Simon & Schuster, xxxii, 133–35, 141–43
small publishing houses, 93–99
smell, new-book, 85
Smith, Charles, 52
Smith, Joy, xxiii–xxiv, xxv, xxxiii, 35–43
Snyder, Dick, 142
social events, 27, 136–37
Sontag, Susan, 151
Stawascz, Cherie, 131, 137–38
Stone for Danny Fisher, A (Robbins), 137
subsidiary rights, xxix–xxx, 100–109
superstores, xxxiii
suppliers, 82–83
Susann, Jacqueline, 150
S. W. Cohen and Associates, 92

tact, 62–63
Talent Art, 75
Tan, Virginia, 66–70
Tebbel, John, 146–47
time, focusing on, 112
"Today Show, The," 137
Tom, Henry, 26
trade paperbacks, xviii, xxix, xxxii–xxxiii,
    25–26
Traveller's Bookstore, xxi, 21
Tulsa, University of, 145
Twayne Publishers, 55
T. Y. Crowell, 89
typefaces, 46, 70, 72, 73
typesetters, xxviii, 49–50, 70–71, 80, 82–83
type specifications, 51, 70–71

University of California Press, 44–45
University of Chicago Press, xxii, 24–29
University of Oklahoma Press, xxii, 29
university presses, xxii, 24–29, 44–45
Unquiet Grave, The (Palinurus), 150

Vaccaro, Claire Naylon, xxvi, 65–73
Vaccaro, Nick, 73
Vassar College, 16
Vaughan, Samuel S., ix–xii
Vaughn, Mary, 60–61
Viscott, David, 141
volunteering, 111, 112
von Mehren, Jane, xxi–xxii, xxxiii, 16–23
Vonnegut, Kurt, 150

Wade, James O'Shea, xxii, 16–20
Walters, Barbara, 137
Washington, University of, 35–36
Wasserman, Marlie, 26–27
White, E. B., 109
Wiar, Kimberly, xxii, 24–29
William Morrow, 57–60
Wilson, Edmund, 146
Wizard of Oz, The, 148
Wolfe, Thomas, 128
Women on Top (Friday), 143
World Publishing Company, xxx, 111–12
Wyatt, Robert B., xxxiii, 145–52

You Can't Go Home Again (Wolfe), 128